MUST
BOOTS

the inside stories of eight Norfolk
men of business in the 19th century

CHRISTOPHER ARMSTRONG

Foreword by Richard Wilson,
Emeritus Professor of History,
University of East Anglia

Norwich Union fire logo 1806

Larks Press

Published by the Larks Press
Ordnance Farmhouse, Guist Bottom
Dereham NR20 5PF
01328 829207
Larks.Press@btinternet.com
Website: www.booksatlarkspress.co.uk

Printed by Short Run Press, Exeter, June 2014

British Library Cataloguing-in-Publication Data
A catalogue record for this book is available
from the British Library

ACKNOWLEDGEMENTS

It would not have been possible to write this book without the help of many people. The staff of the Norfolk Record Office, the Millennium Heritage Centre and Sheringham library have been uniformly helpful and patient in the face of multiple requests for help in locating research material. Archivists Lesley Owen-Edwards (Unilever), and Maria Sienkiewicz and Andrea Waterhouse (both Barclays) have been a great help in locating evidence, as has their opposite number at Aviva, Anna Stone, whose enthusiastic interest has led her to shed light not just on Bignold, but also on others with a less direct Norwich Union connection. Caroline Jarrold and Sir Timothy Colman have offered additional insights into the lives of their ancestors, and a group of 'pressed friends', Richard Crosskill, Michael Brett, and Matthew Morritt, have all read draft chapters and provided helpful, constructive advice. I would like to thank them all, and especially Professor Richard Wilson, not just for gracing this book with a foreword which places the subjects so clearly in context, but also for his advice on the selection of the cast of characters.

ISBN 978 1 904006 73 2

FOREWORD

by Richard Wilson, Emeritus Professor of History, University of East Anglia

When John James wrote his magisterial history of the English worsted industry in 1857 he maintained that Norwich's leading position in it in the mid-eighteenth century entitled it to be compared with Manchester's dominant role in the much larger cotton industry a century later. It was a bold claim on Norwich's behalf for Manchester was the wonder city of Britain's industrial transformation. Indeed Norwich had only very recently given up its claim to Bristol as England's second city. A century later it ranked a mere fourteenth, overtaken by the great industrial cities and ports of the North. The famed Norwich worsted industry, hesitant to mechanise, had slowly declined. By the 1830s it was in crisis. Although there were bright spots in the manufacture of shawls and mourning attire it had handed its supremacy in the more general line of worsted goods to Bradford. In this respect Norwich is an early example of de-industrialisation, its history in the years after 1815, reminiscent in miniature of the general collapse of manufacturing in Britain in the 1980s and 1990s.

Then in the 1850s and 1860s a remarkable revival in the city's fortunes took place. The coming of the railways a little earlier undoubtedly helped as did the growth of banking and insurance, always somewhat shaky and never large employers of labour, for Gurneys Bank and the Norwich Fire and Life Companies were provincial market leaders. Breweries, equally lucrative for their owners, again were never large employers of labour. In Norwich no fewer than four, all with large tied trades, were prominent in the region. But in terms of employment the renaissance of the city's economy in the second half of the nineteenth century was based on shoe-making, food processing and engineering. It was a remarkable transition. Howlett and White's claimed to be the largest shoe

3

factory in England in 1900. In the same year Colman's, already a household name, were the city's leading employer with 2,352 persons working in its mustard manufactory.

The Victorian press loved to explore the enormous contribution men such as J.J. Colman and Sir George White made to Britain's extraordinary predominance. Dense page after page were given over to their lives in business; on their death obituaries were sometimes so extensive that they were reprinted in booklet form. Many of the men, though not all, were self-made, real-life examples of the virtues (faults were glossed over) preached in Samuel Smile's *Self Help* (1859), the classic manual of self-improvement, for many years the next best seller to the Bible and the choice for many a Sunday School prize for good attendance. The importance of religion, often nonconformist, and of paternalistic social responsibility are other themes explored in these popular writings.

Christopher Armstrong has written eight brief, lively biographies of eight men, who laid the ground work of Norwich's economic revival. Not all of them fit Smile's pattern of virtue and self-improvement. Three of them were men of dubious probity. The account we have of Sir Robert Harvey's role in banking would suggest, for some, little changes in that profession. Yet together the sketches provide a timely reminder of the key role they played in the city and its journey from the despair of the second quarter of the nineteenth century to its modest prosperity in the late Victorian and Edwardian periods.

INTRODUCTION

For more than 30 years dating from the late 1870s the citizens of Norwich were able to enjoy a weekly newsletter called *Daylight*, which described itself as Independent, Political, Social and Satirical.

In the early 1900s it included a series of articles about local businesses and their proprietors. To the modern reader these seem devoid of critical appraisal and simply earnest, adulatory (some might say eulogistic) articles about Norwich businesses and their proprietors.

These articles were abridged and gathered together in a single volume by Messrs. E. & W. L. Burgess and published in 1904 under the title *Men Who Have Made Norwich*. The pages are adorned with photographs of the proprietors, their sons, their managers and in some cases the more junior staff of the various businesses described. All of them stare at the camera with that confidence in the permanence of their organisations typical of the high Edwardian era. Sadly, their confidence was misplaced and very few of the businesses survived the turmoil of the twentieth century – many of those that did would probably not be recognisable today to the worthy be-whiskered gentlemen featured in the book.

This book sets out to take a closer, and rather less deferential, look at a few of those whose mark on Norwich in and around the nineteenth century was significant. The choice of characters has been a teasing task. The main criterion has been that the individual must be interesting in his own right, but I have also sought to cover a range of styles from the enlightened Jeremiah James Colman, through the eccentric Thomas Bignold, to the dishonest Sir Robert Harvey. The nature of the companies these men ran is varied. This variety is itself a reflection of Norwich's changing role as its traditional weaving business declined. Financial services are represented both by Bignold's Norwich Union and by Sir

Robert Harvey's Crown Bank, whose failure and subsequent rescue by Gurney's meant that it later became part of Barclays. Manufacturing is represented not just by Colman but also by the inclusion of Sir George White of Howlett and White Shoes, and Albert Caley the mineral water and chocolate magnate. Retailing and publishing, are represented by John Jarrold, weaving and brewing by John Patteson. A little spice is added by the inclusion of Peto, the railway builder, who lived in Norwich for some years and represented it in Parliament.

Many of Norwich's great men of the nineteenth century were simply not quite great enough in a national sense to have attracted the attention of professional biographers. One is sometimes therefore restricted to the uncritical memoirs of sons and daughters, generally privately published, into which no hint of independent comment has been admitted. Happily we are fortunate that in this country we are blessed with a number of commercial organisations that place sufficient value on their own history to maintain comprehensive archives. The material in this book has drawn heavily on the archives in particular of Aviva, Barclays, and Unilever. Other companies who do not have such archives have had sufficient public spirit to deposit historic documents with the Norfolk Record Office or the Millennium Library Heritage Centre. There is much material there for the student of Jarrold & Sons, Norvic, Patteson and Caley. Peto is the one subject in this book who did catch the eye of several biographers, though not especially relating to his work in Norfolk, and they agree about surprisingly little.

At the end of each chapter I have listed the main sources used in drawing these pen pictures; at the end of the book there is a comprehensive bibliography which will, I hope, be of help to anyone wishing to dig a little deeper into the history of any of them, or of Norwich's economic revival in the second half of the nineteenth century.

Work was generally hard at that time. Whether it was the hours worked by Caley's staff in the high season, the crushing routine of working cheek by jowl in a shoe factory or leaving work covered in yellow dust from the manufacture of mustard, there can be little doubt that it was a tough life for the blue collar worker. In *Norwich - A Social Study* published in 1910, the author, C. B. Hawkins, discusses the attraction of watching football:

> 'The average under educated factory operative who has been cramped for six days in the week at his mechanical operation demands the wildest and most thrilling adventures by way of compensation. It is a natural reaction, and is better satisfied in this way than in the public house.'

Perhaps the key words in that quotation are 'under educated' and 'public house'. Three in particular of the businessmen discussed in this book would have strongly endorsed the focus on these. Colman, Jarrold and, in particular, White, had especial concern at the lack of education available to the working classes. Colman funded a school for the children of his employees and Jarrold was responsible for the publication of numerous tracts designed to improve the understanding of the masses. White worked tirelessly to improve educational opportunities; he was not only an educationalist of national importance but also an exceptionally ardent proponent of temperance, as was Jarrold. White, having signed the pledge himself at the age of 17 was responsible for a campaign to try to persuade a million others to follow his example, and became the highly respected President of the Baptist Total Abstinence Association. But even in the factory of one as enlightened as he was, a tough disciplinary regime prevailed; one commentator said that one of his overlookers 'employed methods that would have shamed the overseers on a sugar plantation in the black slavery days'.

As far as the life of white collar workers is concerned, the picture is more variable. Even at Colman's, perhaps the most paternalistic employer of them all, there was a hint of steel; the General Manager apparently practiced the more modern technique of 'managing by walking about' but did so with a knotted rope in his hand, which he would use on any exposed part of the body of a clerk he considered was not working at a satisfactory level. On the other hand, at the Crown Bank, the clerks, between updating heavy ledgers in a fine copperplate, seem to have found time for some amusement. In the archives of Barclay's Bank I found, wrapped in cloth, a collection of sketches drawn by one anonymous member of staff of his colleagues. As one would expect of the age the full set of beard and moustache predominates and respectability is the norm.

Occasionally, when researching, one gets as a treat a special and unexpected distraction. In the next folder I made a delightful discovery – a handwritten volume entitled 'The Rising Son'. Not a spelling mistake, a pun. The volume contained a poem of over seventy stanzas, arranged three to a page and each page headed with a beautifully drawn and coloured cartoon. The subject was the career of a bank clerk, from his father arranging a clerkship for him to his ultimate partnership in the Bank, enabling him (some wishful thinking here) to award an across-the-board pay increase to all the clerical staff. Sadly this work is also anonymous on the part of both poet and artist, although it is clear that they were not one and the same person. The composition, and the artistic skill to adorn it must have meant many hours of surreptitious effort under the noses of the be-whiskered Chief Clerks. Had a Charles Pooter discovered them he would certainly have had palpitations and rushed to tell Mr Perkupp.

Research also has its temptations. Often there are a score of interesting tributaries to the course of the factual stream one is navigating. The problem with these is that they tend to lead away from the intended destination, and they need to be resisted. I surrendered to the siren calls of these tributaries only once. The result is that, in the chapter about Harvey the banker there is an extended section on a Mr Coaks, his solicitor. My excuse is that what makes Coaks interesting is his behaviour in the aftermath of Harvey's suicide, which led eventually to his being struck off. Without the story of Coaks, that of Harvey would be incomplete.

While researching and writing this book a number of features struck me. First, in Norwich, as elsewhere in this period, one cannot but be aware of the importance of committed non-conformists in commercial development. Colman, Jarrold, White and Peto were all prominent Baptists, Caley a member of the Plymouth Brethren. Whether they were driven simply by a huge helping of the Protestant Work Ethic or whether they were motivated by a desire to do God's work by seeking to 'improve' the masses and make the world a better place is the subject of a number of academic papers. I am neither inclined, nor qualified, to add to them, but I suspect that both are true. Perhaps they were still smarting from their relatively recent exclusion from civic office under the Test Acts.

Certainly that would tie in with the second thing that struck me, the extent to which these busy men were prepared to seek civic responsibility, many of them combining the acquisition of great wealth with the assumption of local or national responsibilities. And these were no token appointments. Sir George White for example, served on the Norwich School Board for more than twenty-five years, fifteen as its Chairman, while Patteson was a member of the Corporation for half a century.

The third feature to stand out was the web of connection between so many of the individuals. This goes far beyond coincidence, though that exists as well. Colman and White's partner, Howlett, were baptised on the same day in the same chapel and White was baptised there too, just a year later. The banker, Harvey, followed his father as a director of Bignold's Norwich Union. When Harvey committed suicide it was the Colmans who bought his house. Caley's son bought his from a Jarrold and sold it to the Norwich Union. Colman's purchase of the Carrow site was funded by a loan from the Bignolds. Colman used the railway built by Peto as the first stage in shipping his goods all over the world. Peto attended the same church as Colman and used to give the family a lift back from the service in his private 'omnibus'. White's adult classes were held in a hall built by Peto. Perhaps the strongest link is between Patteson and the Bignolds. Both Patteson and his eldest son served on Norwich Union Boards, and Patteson senior was heavily involved in the process to dismiss Bignold. But the connection went much further. When Patteson fell on hard times he sold his mansion to the Norwich Union as their Head Office, re-named Bignold House, one suspects more for the son, Samuel, than for the father. The Norwich Union also made a substantial loan to him. When Patteson died, despite his son's valiant efforts to pay off his debts, there was still £27,000 outstanding on this loan, equivalent today to more than £2,000,000.

These men often supported the same charities, attended the same churches and worked together in civic affairs. Five sat in Parliament, two, but for Harvey's suicide and the generosity of Patteson's son it could have been four, were adjudged bankrupt. The Harveys and the Pattesons, the two leading Anglican subjects of this book, alternately fell out and made up over several generations on matters both political and military. Despite this, Patteson backed the Harveys in their successful bid to gain the valuable role of collecting Land Tax on the failure of the (related) Kerrisons. Peto and Harvey were made Baronets, Colman declined the same honour, and White was knighted. In the nineteenth century, perhaps before and beyond as well, Norwich was dominated by a small clique of merchant families.

Almost all the characters had significant and attractive qualities. For all their hard work and apparent moral rectitude, some of them had warts as well – and sometimes it is these that make them interesting. This book does not set out to provide a full biography of these individuals – it is more by way of a reflection of a lost Norwich exposed by reference to them. I have appended a postscript to each of the lives, with the exception of Peto, to show what has happened to the organisation since the events described. These are generally quite brief, except in the case of John Jarrold. Jarrold & Sons is certainly a company that would be recognisable to John Jarrold even today, and with the seventh generation of the family still involved in its management, it merits a more detailed explanation.

C. S. Armstrong
Bodham, 2014

CONTENTS

Sir Robert Harvey Bt (1817-1870)
Banker, Member of Parliament and speculator – and his solicitor, Isaac Bugg Coaks

'A mean sod who is afraid to risk his money bags by taking part in politics, tho' he wants to be a bar[one]t to gratify his petty vanity.'

John Wodehouse,
First Earl of Kimberley

September 12th 1862 was a beautiful sunny day and thousands came by special train to Crown Point, the home of banker Robert Harvey, to witness a Military Review. The atmosphere was festive. Among the visitors was a Norfolk parson, who was taking his daughter out for a treat.

In his diary he recorded the nature of the military manoeuvres – 'very tame', the cavalry gallop (Mr Hay Gurney's Mounted Volunteers) 'no one knew whether it was a gallant charge or an ignominious defeat' – and at the review he seemed more impressed with the entertainment, an 'aeronaut' in a yellow balloon, a French giant, a certain M. Breze who was 8 ft 6 inches tall, and who, accompanied by a dwarf, toured the tables of the giant marquee in which several thousand guests were wined and dined at Harvey's expense. The food and wine were of excellent quality. The afternoon was devoted to pleasure, with horse racing for the officers, Punch and Judy for the children and a number of bands for the benefit of all. As night fell there was a grand display of fireworks.

Writing in his diary, the parson reviewed the day. What was Harvey's motive for this remarkable generosity? Was he planning to stand for Parliament, or had he just decided to upstage Lord Leicester, who had held a similar event at Holkham the previous year? In any event, he reported that some believed simply that Harvey just had so much money he didn't know what to do with it. His first thought proved correct - Sir Robert *was* planning to stand for parliament – he stood, unsuccessfully, for Thetford the following year, but was elected in 1865.

Less than 8 years later, on Saturday the 16th July 1870 a notice appeared on the door of Harvey's Crown Bank:

'In consequence of the lamentable catastrophe which has happened to Sir Robert Harvey, it has been determined by the other partners to suspend the business of the Bank for the present.'

The previous afternoon Mrs Lambart, the sister-in-law of Sir Robert, whose wife was holidaying in Lowestoft, was taking a stroll through the same grounds of Crown Point that had been the site of the Military Review, when she discovered Sir Robert, lying under an ash tree, shot through the chest. With a plank as a makeshift stretcher, he was carried by some workmen back into the house. When discovered, he was conscious, reportedly 'shifting himself' onto the plank, and instructing the workers to 'go steadily, or I shall be dead before you get to the house'.

Rumours quickly spread. A letter written on the 18th, refers to an initial suspicion that Sir Robert had been shot by his son, but that it appeared later that he had shot himself, apparently missing with the first two shots. The writer of the letter (to her brother-in-law) was Mrs Buxton, the wife of banker Samuel Gurney Buxton, later the first Chairman of Barclays. She sounded almost thrilled at the excitement of it all. In a flurry of exclamation marks she described how, on the 15th she had been holding a Village Missionary Meeting on the lawn of her home, Catton Hall, when it was interrupted by the arrival of Mr Birkbeck, a partner in the bank, who reported that Sir Robert had been shot by, it was rumoured, his son. A servant was sent to Crown Point to verify the story but was turned away. Then, at 5 a.m. the next day, she was woken by a knocking at the door. The early visitor was a Mr Mottram[1] from the Bank, who had come to tell her husband that he had heard from Cooks (sic), the lawyer, that 'Harvey had smashed'. The news was accompanied by a fearsome thunderstorm and her husband hurried away to meet his partners at 6.00 a.m. It wasn't until lunchtime that she had confirmation that 'Harvey's had closed'. Meanwhile her husband had gone to London – the process of taking over the liabilities of the Crown Bank was under way even though, at the time, it was expected that Sir Robert would survive. But he did not, dying on the 19th with his bank's liabilities some 60% greater than its assets. Ironically, the Parish Clothing Fund of the parson who had visited the Review was just one of the estimated 3,000 depositors who lost money.

The inquest was held with almost indecent haste the following day in Sir Robert's own morning room. Nudged by the Coroner, Mr W. N. H. Turner, who opened the proceedings by declaring that there was no doubt that the deceased had died from a pistol shot having, 'in all probability, been fired by his own hand' the jury took the hint and quickly determined that he had shot himself during a period of 'temporary insanity'. Medical evidence was offered that he was an excitable man with a 'strong tendency to mental disorder'. His solicitor, a Mr Coaks, believed that he had 'inherited insanity'. Evidence that the pistol had been found some distance from Sir Robert and confirmation that there were indeed, as suggested in Mrs Buxton's letter, three empty chambers in the pistol, did not seem to cause anyone to express doubt about the verdict, although one juror did ask to see the weapon. Evidence was offered that it had been bought by Sir Robert himself, and had been in the care of his brother-in-law, Capt. Lambart who had left the gun locked up while he was away. It later transpired that when Sir Robert had purchased the pistol from a Norwich gunsmith, he had fired two trial shots, perhaps explaining the other empty chambers.

What had led to the transformation from ostentatious public gestures to the collapse of his bank was not just wanton extravagance but a combination of speculation, dishonesty, and, presumably, weak audit trails.

The final straw was a demand for an additional £200,000 by his brokers. Sir Robert, it transpired, had for a decade been speculating on the stock exchange, funding his investments by transfers from Bank funds disguised in the accounts as a series of loans made to fictitious customers. The market, spooked by the imminent outbreak of war between France and Prussia, went against him and the game was up. The result was to bring down the bank – and his two partners, innocent if naïve victims of his actions. A number of accounts of the affair attribute his losses to his having backed the losing side in the war, but since war was not declared until a few days after the shooting, in fact on the day of his death, these appear mistaken. But the markets were in a jittery state and it was reported in the press that Harvey had 'engaged in financial operations, and rumours are current, which it is feared may be well-founded, that his present deplorable aberration has resulted from excitement caused by the violent speculative changes of the past week'.

Sir Robert was the son of a distinguished man, Major General Sir Robert Harvey, Wellington's liaison officer with the Portuguese during the Peninsular War, who, having married his cousin, inherited a substantial estate from her father. Obviously he relished recalling his days in the Peninsular War, as he named the farms on his estate after some of the battles. When he died, in 1860, he left £350,000 to his son. Not enough, clearly, to satisfy a voracious appetite for speculative investment. Robert was the eldest of the three sons of the Major General to survive infancy. The second was John, born 5 years later, in 1822 and the third Edward Kerrison, born in 1826. Both brothers have a part in the story, though not as active participants. John was the beneficiary of a relatively small settlement of £5,000. It seems probable that he was the cause of the belief that there was insanity in the family. Described in 1872 as 'having been for many years, of weak mind' he lived at Tharston Hall and, in the 1854 White's Directory, there is listed at the same address one John Mears, described as 'servant to the idiot'.

Edward Kerrison Harvey played a major, if involuntary, role in the later stages of the story. He was born with a medical condition and his father left him a life interest in assets producing an income of £13,000 p.a. On Edward Kerrison's death, the capital was to go to the eldest surviving son, Robert. The latter, always a man with a keen eye for a bargain, purchased the life interest for £60,000, equal to a little less than five years income from the settlement. This asset became an important part of Robert's estate and what happened to it after his suicide was, as will be seen, a very significant aspect of litigation which stretched on for more than twenty-five years after his death.

Harvey & Hudson's Bank had been established in 1792 when Robert John Harvey, a worsted manufacturer, joined forces with a Mr Hudson, who had been banking with a different partner for fourteen years. This sort of diversification into alternative fields was typical of the time; Bignold's Norwich General Insurance and Patteson's brewery were other examples. Harvey died in 1816; his elder son, also Robert, died, childless, just 4 years later, being succeeded as a partner by his younger brother and by his nephew the Major General, who had retired from the Army at the end of the Peninsular War. The Major General remained a partner in the Bank for 40 years. Banking was in his blood as his mother was herself the daughter of another banker, Sir Robert Kerrison. The Kerrisons became an important part of the Crown Bank story. Their bank had failed in 1808, but not before it had acquired the extremely lucrative responsibility for the collection of land tax in Norfolk. When they failed, this responsibility became that of Harvey & Hudson. The benefit it entailed was the retention of a capital balance of something in the order of £30,000 on a continuous basis without having to pay interest to obtain it. At the time of the failure of Crown Bank, two members of the Kerrison family were partners – both were to be bankrupted by the practices of Sir Robert.

Crown Bank (as Harvey & Hudson became) seemed a model institution. It appeared well run, and it attracted prestigious customers. The Harveys had long been a prominent local family – members of the family had been Mayor of Norwich on no less than eight occasions in the 18th century. Both Sir Robert and his father were Directors of the Norwich Union, Sir Robert represented a Norfolk constituency at Westminster, his father the Major General was a JP and Deputy Lieutenant of Norfolk. The Bank had moved in 1866 to palatial premises, built for Sir Robert to a design by the London architect, Philip Hardwick, at a cost of £30,000. The building was, and remains, an imposing structure, complete with Ionic columns and balustraded terraces. Since the demise of the Bank it has served successively as Norwich's General Post Office (witnessing the earliest use of post codes, Norwich being the pilot city), studios for Anglia Television and now as the Norwich office of Savills Estate Agents. In 1866 it must have seemed to embody just that solidarity needed to reinforce the confidence of customers.

In recent times the Bank had developed a network of about 30 branches, mostly in the market towns of East Anglia. Some of the managers obviously followed the senior partner in sponsoring public events, if not on the scale of the1862 military review. The diary of the parson who had attended the military review recorded, in January 1859, that

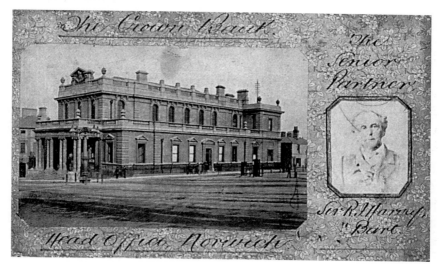

Crown Bank, later the General Post Office

the Dereham manager of the Bank, a Mr Lane, had given 'a gratuitous concert to the town & neighbourhood in the Corn Hall, his object being a patriotic desire to improve the public taste. The performers were a section of the Norwich Harmonic Society. An uglier set of used up looking musical hacks I never saw' he concluded.

The sudden closure of such an apparently robust and public-spirited institution caused consternation. Saturday was market day, and the day on which wages were normally paid. Mr Buxton and his partners, having been roused at 5 in the morning responded with great energy. Their bank, Messrs Gurneys, Birkbecks, Barclay & Buxton immediately announced that they would advance half the balance held in accounts at Crown Bank, thus enabling customers of the Bank to manage the immediate impact and pay the wages due that day. They declined, however to honour banknotes issued by Harvey's Bank.

The very same day petitions in bankruptcy were presented jointly in the names of Harvey and the two Kerrisons. Following Harvey's death fresh petitions were presented on the 21st July and both Kerrisons were declared bankrupt the following day.

We have become only too accustomed to the long drawn out process of resolving the problems of banks in the 21st century, so the pace at which events developed in the 19th seems electric. By July 20th, the day after Sir Robert's death, *The Times* was able to announce that the business of Crown Bank 'had been taken over by Gurney's.' The total price was £42,000, half for the goodwill, and half for the premises, a provisional agreement having been reached between Gurneys and Harvey's solicitor, Mr Coaks, as early as the evening of the 18th, while Harvey was still alive.

That part of the process may have been prompt, but the repercussions of the failure rolled on for many years. It was not, of course, just the Harvey family who were involved. Indeed, Sir Charles, Harvey's eldest surviving son, who inherited the baronetcy originally conferred on his father just two years before his death, was left sufficiently comfortably off to be able to purchase Rainthorpe Hall, a magnificent Elizabethan country house, where he lived with his first wife, whom he had married shortly before the Bank failed. He had benefited from the fact that the bulk of the Harvey estate was entailed, his father having only a life interest.

Like his grandfather he became a JP and he reached the rank of Colonel in the Army. There is no clear evidence to substantiate the rumour to which Mrs Gurney had referred that he had shot his father, and there is no evidence that there had been a falling out between father and son, despite a reference to the latter's 'disgraceful marriage' in a local diary.

For many others, the future was not so fortunate. A number of brokers who had been handling Sir Robert's affairs themselves failed, but the biggest losers, apart from the customers, were the Kerrisons. Kerrison, senior, had taken no part, and, it seemed, little interest, in the work of the Bank, having declined an invitation to become a partner some time before. However, Sir Robert on becoming the sole partner approached him again, and he consented, possibly hoping to help facilitate an arrangement whereby his son Roger was offered a career within the Bank. Roger's own work for the Bank involved him in dealing with the Bank's agents, travelling extensively and he was generally in the office only on Saturdays. A book published in 1900 referred to 'elaborate precautions taken by Sir Robert to prevent him [Roger] from being acquainted with the way in which he was employing Bank funds in speculation', and it seems probable that he really was unaware. The result of the failure was that he was not only bankrupted but also suffered a loss of the means of earning his living.

His condition was such that he applied for the Secretary-ship of the Bank of Bengal based in Calcutta. To support his application he asked Birkbeck, one of Gurney's partners for a reference. His correspondence with Mr Birkbeck highlights his condition. His only income is £300 p.a. from his wife's marriage settlement; the salary for the Calcutta role is £3,000 and a house. While he does not have any great expectation that he will be given the job, he does have some connection with a number of those on the selection committee, and the previous incumbent, Mr George Dickson, who was 'likely to be consulted as to his successor' was a friend of his father-in-law. Unfortunately for Roger Kerrison, connections and reference didn't cut sufficient ice and the Bank appointed a Mr Hardie, an existing employee who had acted as Secretary in an interim capacity. Kerrison's appeal to Mr Birkbeck did not, however fall on deaf ears – he was appointed to a clerkship in Gurney's Bank, and in due course became a partner in Gurneys, Alexander & Co. in Ipswich.

Acceptance of the story that the Kerrisons were but innocent dupes seems implicit in the payments approved by a creditors' meeting in December 1873, chaired by Sir Samuel Bignold, the Secretary of Norwich Union, of £1,000 and £500 respectively to Kerrison Senior and Junior, in recognition of their help in the proceedings. This was generous; by that time it was becoming clear that little would be forthcoming from Sir Robert's personal estate. There was little to cheer at the meeting, though the announcement that amongst the irrecoverable sums from Sir Robert's estate was some £10,000 that had been advanced to 'certain persons in Thetford', presumably costs incurred in connection with his election (see below) was reported to have been greeted with laughter.

In fact, the person who was to be involved longest and most deeply in the sequel to the failure had been, thus far, a fringe figure, Isaac Bugg Coaks, Harvey's solicitor. It is sometimes said that, in these affairs, it is the lawyers who are enriched by the troubles of others, and Isaac Bugg Coaks made a great deal of hay. Too much hay; eventually he was struck off the Rolls for what was found to be 'gross impropriety' in relation to this case.

Coaks was a remarkable man who, from humble beginnings, became extremely rich and achieved a degree of social recognition unusual in a man of his background. The son of the village carpenter in the village of Brundall, Isaac Bugg, as he was born, married a Miss Fussey, who later, inherited from her uncle, a Mr Coaks. Bugg decided to adopt the name.

Already, at the creditors' meeting referred to above, there was some concern at Coaks's behaviour, and he sought to justify his costs and those of Mr Bailey, the trustee in bankruptcy. There is also, in the archive of Barclays Bank, what appears to be an office note made by the Commissioner in Bankruptcy, listing a series of payments under the heading 'Information is required concerning the payments made to Mr I. B. Coaks by Messrs Gurney & Co. For what consideration, and on whose behalf were the respective payments

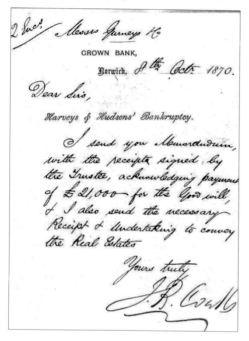

made?' The note is undated, but the payments listed arose in 1870 and 1871, which suggests that eyebrows were being raised very early on. Mr Bailey had been acting for one of Harvey's biggest creditors, a Mr Gedge, but his appointment as Trustee had been instigated by Coaks, and this was an issue which later became important.

Creditor concern continued. It was widely known that the property at Crown Point had been sold to the Colmans for £55,000, but there were unanswered questions about other assets, such as the life interest Harvey had bought from his brother. It transpired that Coaks had personally bought a number of Harvey's assets, including, as a member of a syndicate, that life interest in Edward Kerrison Harvey. The syndicate, which included Coaks, Bailey and Sir Samuel Bignold's nephew, a Mr Bunyon, who was the Actuary at Norwich Union, paid £40,000.

Apart from other personal creditors, there was also a legal issue with regard to the £600,000 Harvey had misappropriated from the Bank. Sir Robert having taken the money and speculated it away, the question arose as to whether his estate should be liable for this, having received no benefit, or whether his private creditors should take precedence. The lawyers probably rubbed their hands, and well they might. The ensuing cases involved no less than twelve QCs with total costs exceeding £60,000.

By 1880, the suspicion that something was amiss had grown to the extent that graffiti saying 'Crown Bank Robbery' or 'Bank Swindle' were not unusual. In that year, two creditors decided to take some action – it was, after all, ten years since Sir Robert's death. The two, Mr Boswell and Mr Baxter, instructed their lawyer to investigate the purchase of the life interest, and followed up with a civil action[2] for fraud. They alleged that Coaks, holding a position of trust, shouldn't have bought the life interest, and that similar considerations should apply also to Mr Bailey. Further that the syndicate had underpaid, having achieved a discounted price by disguising the true state of Edward Kerrison Harvey's (EKH) health. Mr Bunyon, the Norwich Union actuary had become involved because the company advanced most of the purchase money, requiring a life assurance policy on EKH as security. They were also alleged to have misled the Court of Chancery in seeking consent for the sale by providing an insurance quotation the terms of which were worse than those actually available, and to have paid an alternative bidder to desist.

It turned out that Coaks, perhaps anticipating such allegations, had obtained the consent of the Master of the Rolls before completing the purchase, and the case went against the creditors. This result didn't deflect from Coaks and his colleagues suffering in terms of reputation, and, in 1884, the Court of Appeal reversed the original decision, describing the syndicate's behaviour as 'a wicked fraud'.

By now, the lawyers were in full cry, and in 1885, the House of Lords overturned the Court of Appeal's decision, saying the fraud had not been proved. By then Baxter had died, but Boswell tried again in 1892. He failed again but another appeal was heard in the House of Lords in 1894. This time fresh evidence was adduced: a shorthand note of a letter dictated by Coaks to Bunyon in 1872, from which it appeared clear that Coaks had known that insurance was available on EKH's life on better terms than had been admitted, thus implying a greater life expectancy than that implicit in the price paid.

Sadly for the persistent Boswell, it was held that the note itself did not constitute sufficient evidence to prove the fraud, and the syndicate won again. It was, however, enough to alert the Official Receiver, Mr Gould, as Trustee in Bankruptcy of Harvey's Bank, who took action against Coaks and the executors of Bailey, who had died. He alleged that Coaks had held on to funds to which he was not entitled, had profited by re-selling assets he had bought from Harvey's estate and that Coaks had made exaggerated expense claims.

The case was brought on evidence supplied by a mole in Coaks's office, a Mr Clarke. Clarke, it transpired, had sought to blackmail Coaks by threatening to disclose the evidence. Coaks had refused to pay and sought to protect himself by writing to the Receiver saying that an error in his claims had just come to light, amounting to just £524.

Initially, this ploy seemed to have done the trick, but Clarke brought even more evidence and Gould instituted a Board of Trade examination. This examination unearthed 'laxity and dishonesty' in the way Coaks had dealt with client funds. Money received had been banked but not distributed until claimed. As many were in ignorance of the receipt of money they didn't claim, and the funds were later re-credited to Coaks's personal account. They also concluded that there had been impropriety when Coaks purchased for himself assets from the Harvey estate and Coaks was required to return that to which he was not entitled, though this did not include the income received from the purchase of the life interest.

All this was too much for the Law Society who, in 1896, brought eight charges against Coaks. He was able to deflect some, but he was adjudged secretly to have shared fees with Bailey, to have charged for work done by Bailey, misappropriated funds, secretly purchased assets from the Harvey estate, and double charged on expenses.

These were variously treated as professional misconduct and, in one case, gross professional misconduct, and he was struck off the Rolls. The conclusion was reported thus in the *Solicitor's Journal and Reporter*: 'The facts are clear. He, and the Trustee, Bailey, concerted, each using his influence for the other, that the one should be appointed the Trustee and the other should be appointed the solicitor, and that they should share in equal moieties whatever was made out of the estate either in respect of solicitor's costs or in respect of trustee's remuneration.'

Despite this decision Coaks didn't forfeit the income from the life interest. EKH turned out to be far less of a creaking gate than had been anticipated and survived for more than 30 years after Coaks and colleagues purchased the life interest, They turned their £40,000 investment into about £400,000 in total. This aspect was picked up as far away as New Zealand where, on Coaks's death a press article with the headline:

£470,000 for £40,000. ONE TIME OFFICE BOY'S
AMAZING COUP

related the story, if in an exaggerated way; Coaks had not been the sole recipient of the £13,000 a year. The report concluded with what it asserted to be 'an amusing story' which it carefully described – perhaps lest the late Mr Coaks might remain litigious from the grave – as 'no doubt untrue'. It was to the effect that Coaks, whose appearance was said to be rendered 'sinister' by the loss of one eye, had, in the course of cross-examination in court been asked by counsel whether another party in the case was not his 'alter ego'.

Coaks was said to have had later to ask his own counsel the meaning of the phrase, and, on being told that it could be translated as 'your other eye' had promptly taken umbrage at the perceived attempt to make fun of his appearance.

Coaks died in 1910, still a wealthy man. He had bought large amounts of property and his estate was worth over £400,000, roughly £40 million in the terms of value in 2012.

He was certainly an astute man, avaricious, not over-scrupulous, focussed, driven and arrogant. That he was cunning is clear from both his application to the Master of the Rolls, and his later partial admission to Gould. One senses that his satisfaction at the wealth he had accumulated would have meant more to him than the disgrace of his disbarment. It would have pleased him that his story was known on the other side of the globe. The details of his will appeared in the Australian press under the headline:

'£415,000 LEFT BY A VILLAGE CARPENTER'S SON'

One suspects he would have revelled in the disclosure of the amount, if not in that of his origins.

As for Harvey, his character is not so easy to assess from available evidence, but there are a few clues. His election to Parliament was apparently managed by an agent, one E. N. Cole, who found the experience rather costly. In a lengthy petition to Gurney's Bank following the collapse of Crown Bank, he described how he had been summoned by Harvey in 1863 to manage Harvey's election at Thetford, how he'd warned him that it would not be easy, and how, after Harvey's defeat by 11 votes, he had put in 'seven years of hard work' on Harvey's behalf. He had advised Harvey to buy all the property of voteable value in the vicinity that he could, take over all the mortgages he could, and grant loans to voters. Where he couldn't buy the houses, he should hire them, improve them and then sublet them to suitable, supportive, tenants. He should involve himself with local

27

charities, hold a Fête, arrange outings for the voters, and ensure that the Voting Register, apparently in a poor state, was updated and its maintenance properly overseen. Harvey instructed Cole to do all this for him, and offered the services of a clerk from Norwich to do Cole's other work, freeing him to work exclusively for Harvey. Having followed his instructions and reported weekly to Harvey, Cole felt he had been instrumental in Harvey's success in the 1865 election. Despite Harvey being ill on election day, Cole had been able, when the result was known, to see Harvey with the doctor's consent. Harvey had expressed his pleasure and promised to place a substantial sum to the credit of Cole by way of payment. He didn't. Cole remained unpaid five years later when Harvey died. To rub salt into the wound, Cole claimed that he had been made to pay for the time of Harvey's clerk out of his own pocket, and had been charged interest by the bank of nearly £800 on the expenditure he had undertaken on Harvey's behalf.

All this was set out in a beautiful hand, running to many pages. Whether Cole's plea to the Gurneys, as the purchasers of Crown Bank, was successful is not clear, but the incident does suggest that Harvey was ambitious – his brief sojourn in Parliament was marked by the creation of the baronetcy – willing to spend large sums on property purchase to gain votes and achieve his ambition, yet too mean to pay his agent. Cole put his losses at about £2,500 – chickenfeed to Harvey, but not to Cole.

Much of this is borne out by an entry in the journal of John Wodehouse, First Earl of Kimberley, dated 22nd November 1862. Describing how Harvey had first called on him on the 31st October to ask to be recommended to Lord Palmerston for a baronetcy, Wodehouse went on to record that Harvey had boasted of his wealth and influence and said that he was not anxious to become involved in politics but that he would if he had to in order, as Wodehouse put it, 'to force his way into the dignity he covets'. Wodehouse declined to make such recommendation, not least because he was a Liberal and Harvey a Tory. But Harvey wouldn't take 'no' for an answer and wrote again on the 22nd November, sending a petition for such an honour to Queen Victoria, which he asked Wodehouse to forward to Palmerston. Wodehouse declined again, and couldn't resist the temptation to record disdainfully that Harvey had arrived at the lodge in a 'fly' and walked up to the house rather than be seen arriving in such an undistinguished form of transport. 'This little incident', recorded Wodehouse, 'describes the mean vulgarity of the man better than volumes'.

He was clearly acquisitive. The original Harvey estates had been entailed, so that he had only a life interest. He set out determinedly to buy further land in his own right. By the time of his death he owned the whole of Whitlingham Village, and large parts of the neighbouring Trowse – well over 2,500 acres in all. He was socially ambitious, High Sheriff for Norfolk in 1863, MP for Thetford in 1865, created Baronet in 1868 – all of these arising during the time he was using the Bank's funds to speculate. It is ironical that his family motto was *Alteri si tibi* – 'To another as to thyself' – or, in more modern usage 'Do unto others as you would have them do to you'.

He was, of course, dishonest, but whether he was a gambler, or simply convinced that he could beat the market we shall never know. There is little evidence to suggest insanity - perhaps the merest hint in the fact that Capt. Lambart had locked the gun away, maybe anticipating a catastrophe. Harvey had been contemplating the purchase of a gun for a while. He had tried and rejected several pistols before buying, and when he did, he arranged for the weapon to be delivered to him personally at the back door of the bank. It could be argued that expecting to get away with such wholesale fraud was insanity, but get away with it he did for a decade, and if war had been averted he might have continued to do so.

Postscript

Some of the Gurneys had had their own troubles, the discount house Overend, Gurney and Co. having gone into liquidation just four years before Harvey's Bank. This resulted in the criminal prosecution of the Directors for having made false statements in the Prospectus issued when they made a share offering in 1865. The Directors were acquitted, the Lord Chief Justice concluding they were guilty only of 'grave error' but not criminality. Gurney's Bank in Norwich survived – at a price – and, in 1896, joined with several others to become Barclay's Bank.

[1] Mottram was an old and trusted employee – the second of three generations of the same family to serve the bank. He had been a school-friend of Bartlett Gurney. One of the roles of Mottram's father had been the transportation of specie to and from London by coach. This was a dangerous task – a letter by Hay Gurney many years earlier had referred to a journey undertaken by Mottram carrying £80,000 with the comment 'I cannot but think of it as a very dangerous cargo to have care of'. These concerns were later borne out when on another such journey, a highwayman made three attempts to stop the coach. As he approached for the third pass one of the other passengers spotted that the highwayman was holding something with a metallic glint which he took to be a gun, and shot him dead. When the coach stopped it turned out that the 'gun' was in fact a brass candlestick. It later transpired that the highwayman had, in collusion with the driver, tried this trick three times before, successfully. The Mottram who brought the news of Harvey to the Buxtons had himself in earlier days carried out similar deliveries, once expressing himself as relieved that it was empty-handed, on the return journey, that he found himself in the company of someone he didn't like the look of. His fellow passenger was one James Blomfield Rush, hanged at Norwich Castle for one of the most renowned murders of the Victorian era.

[2] A relatively painless way of following the very complex story of the various trials is by reference to *Norfolk Annals*, by Charles Mackie, 1801 – 1850, a series of extracts from the *Norfolk Chronicle*.

Sources:

Annals of an East Anglian Bank – see Bibliography
Daily News, Perth, 5th September 1910
Death and Disgrace in Victorian Norwich – see Bibliography
History of the Bank of Bengal – see Bibliography
London Gazette September 2nd 1870
London Gazette, June 21st 1872
New Zealand Herald 19th February 1910
Norwich Heritage Economic and Regeneration Trust website www.heritagecity.org
Norwich since 1550 –see Bibliography
The Journal of John Wodehouse, see Bibliography
The Story of Norwich – see Bibliography
The Times Archive Material in the archives of Barclays Bank
Under the Parson's Nose – see Bibliography

Thomas Bignold (1761-1835)
founder of Norwich Union, Eccentric and Bankrupt

'It was Unanimously Resolved that Mr Thomas Bignold Senior be now removed and dismissed from the situation of Secretary to the Society.'

Such was a resolution passed by the Board of Norwich Union at a Special General Meeting at the Angel Inn, Norwich on the 9th November 1818.

This was the beginning of the end of an extraordinary career. By the time he died, in 1835, Bignold had been charged with perjury, imprisoned for debt, declared bankrupt, and had patented the invention of revolving heels for ladies shoes; happily, he had also got back on reasonable terms with his sons, whom he blamed for his dismissal. More importantly, despite his many idiosyncrasies, he had been the moving force behind the successful establishment of what became one of the biggest insurance companies in Europe, with worldwide connections, still going strong two centuries after he set it up.

The most surprising thing about his dismissal is, perhaps, that it didn't happen earlier. To describe his relationship with the Board as 'fraught' would be a massive understatement. To understand why, it is necessary to go back to the very beginning, though the first signs of difficulty didn't occur until 1805.

On April 13th that year, *The Norwich Mercury* carried the following item:

> T. Bignold took up the firepan and tongs, and placing himself on a chair, declared that he would break the head of the first man that attempted to open the chest, and, calling on his son, John Cocksedge Bignold, desired him to get his pistol which he immediately did and, presenting it, threatened in a most positive manner to fire at any of the Directors who should attempt to open the chest; the father at the same time encouraging his son to fire, saying 'Fire, John – I will protect you!' Finding both father and son apparently determined to make use of their weapons against them, the Directors thought it most prudent to withdraw from the office.

Such at least was the version of events the directors caused to be published in the press, together with a notice describing Bignold as 'the late Secretary' of the company, and stressing that, in future, no payments for the company should be made to him, but rather to an attorney appointed by the directors. The incident followed a meeting held on April 1st in a public house in Norwich when Bignold refused to make available to the directors the books detailing the state of the business.

Yet another notice appeared on the same day, but this time at the instigation of Bignold, taking full credit for the establishment and achievements of Norwich Union, and claiming that he had tried to take measures 'to prevent irregularities in the management of the funds of the Society'. He went on to complain that the directors had procured attendees at the Society's General Meeting who had acted in a disorderly way, demanding his dismissal by acclamation. Bignold said that he had refused to let the directors open the box because he believed they intended to 'carry off' the papers. Just 'another day at the office' for this most eccentric, if energetic, of entrepreneurs.

The cause of the argument and its sequel require an understanding of Bignold's background, personality and business acumen. Originally from Kent, Bignold was the son of a tenant farmer. His early career had been as an exciseman. It isn't clear why he moved to Norfolk but, having done so, he married Sarah Long, a widow, who had continued to run her first husband's grocery shop after his death. Bignold successfully expanded the business into the wine and hop trade, and became a model citizen, acting as churchwarden and achieving a reputation as a competent businessman. He and Sarah had six children in as many years. He might have settled down as a mildly prosperous, respected lower middle-class pillar of the city, but his was too restless and too ambitious a nature to do anything of the sort.

Bignold's great great grandson, Sir Robert Bignold, in his book describing his family's connection with Norwich Union skates carefully around some aspects of Thomas's life and career where the water is particularly murky and the ice particularly thin, but he relates the family tradition that Thomas decided to found an insurance company because he had been unable to get insurance for the removal of his goods by coach from Kent to Norfolk. Such was the corporate acceptance of this delightfully romantic story that when, 200 years later, Norwich Union finally broke with Thomas's commitment to mutuality and floated on the stock-market, the original share certificates bore illustrations both of Bignold and of a coach in recognition of the story.

Bignold had established Norwich Union on a mutual basis. This meant that the company was owned by its policyholders who would benefit from any profit made. Instead of shareholders receiving a dividend, policyholders would receive a bonus, initially after seven years, when the extent of the company's progress was clearer. Many insurers, and of course building societies, were established on a mutual basis and in relatively recent times their members (i.e. their policyholders or depositors) have benefited further from this automatic ownership by way of 'free' shares as some of those institutions concluded that mutuality was no longer the best route for them. The wish to be able to raise capital when needed meant that, for some, it had become more attractive to be listed on the stockmarket.

Norwich Union's own demutualisation 200 years after its foundation enabled such access. It seems ironic that the share certificates issued on demutualisation should have borne an image of such a champion of mutuality as Bignold. Some might also question whether portraying on the share certificate a man eventually imprisoned for debt and declared bankrupt was the most obvious way to gain confidence in the market.

Sadly, the coach insurance story is probably apocryphal. Thomas's first involvement with the insurance business was with the Norwich General, a company not founded until he had been in Norwich nearly a decade. In any event, although he was its first Secretary, he was not its instigator.

Insurance was hardly a mature market; many people had no cover so the scope for growing such a business was immense. The market had until then been dominated by London-based companies, but in several parts of the country local businessmen were seeking to develop alternatives. There were several reasons for this. First, local magnates were anxious to spread their own risk. The protection offered by running one's own business on a limited liability basis lay a long time in the future and there was some comfort in diversifying so that one's eggs were spread over a number of baskets. Second, as far as Norwich was concerned, it was an area where local underwriting of insurance, at least of local property, seemed feasible. Relatively low valuations limited the size of risk, as did the diffuse nature of the textile industry which was spread through many home-based operations. This meant that premium rates could challenge those charged in London. Those local magnates who were of this view decided to establish their own Fire Insurance Company and back it financially. They established the Norwich General Assurance Company in 1792, and, seeking a man to run it, chose Bignold.

He may seem a strange choice – after all he had no experience of insurance – but that was seen as no impediment, and he was not the only novice to be given such a position. The role of 'Secretary' was a wide one, he would be expected to develop the business, to deal with the financial operation of the company and to manage the administration. One can reasonably infer that Bignold's record as a small businessman and the experience of detail he had gained as an exciseman were seen to qualify him for the role. Rates could be fixed by adjusting those charged by the London companies, and, by restricting cover financially to £3,000 and, in terms of location, to the surrounding area, his lack of underwriting experience was rendered less important. Also he was a candidate likely to be acceptable to both the nonconformist Whig and the Anglican Tory wings of the founding group, having not yet alienated either.

It was a low-key start. Bignold continued to run his existing business, now with his brother as a partner. Initially, the new company operated from his existing retail premises on Gentleman's Walk, close to stationers, drapers and the cutlery shop where Parson Woodforde bought his razors. The new insurance business grew quite quickly, despite the concentration on local sources, and it was successful, delivering profit and a good dividend stream.

Bignold was ambitious; it was clear from the start that he placed a value on good marketing and competitive pricing. The approach of the directors, of steady and local development, was never likely to satisfy the drive and ambition of a man like Bignold. Five years after the company started, he left without warning.

He had clearly planned his departure carefully, if secretly. Within a month, he had established the Norwich Union. Without access to those local businessmen who had funded Norwich General, Bignold needed to find another way to establish the business. The route he took involved twenty-eight policyholders (including himself) each providing a guarantee of £1,000 to create a reserve. Mutuality was really his only option; his abrupt departure from the Norwich General had alienated those most likely, and able, to invest in a new enterprise.

Bignold's energy was manifest in all he did. He was a man of imagination, astute, forceful – on occasion excessively so – and extremely ambitious. He was also a very skilled manipulator. His ambition knew no limits and the force of his personality enabled him to establish Norwich Union on a basis that offered him the prospect of great financial return for little risk. In fixing his own remuneration he established a package that placed the emphasis solely on the volume, rather than the quality, of business – hardly a desirable basis for an insurer. His remuneration was, quite simply, to be 10 per cent of all premiums received, regardless of profitability. When, later, Life Assurance was added to the mix, he was paid 10 per cent of the first year's premium and 5 per cent of each subsequent one. Further the Deed of Settlement establishing the Society contained a clause to the effect that Bignold could be dismissed only if the majority of members at a General Meeting voted for his dismissal. This limited the options for the directors in the event of their dissatisfaction with his performance, and gave Bignold substantial freedom to run the business along whatever lines he chose.

His strategy was, from the start, one of growth. Premiums grew so fast that, by 1815 he was enjoying a gross income of about £10,000 p.a. half from Life and half from Fire. To put this in perspective one can take as a point of reference the immensely wealthy Mr Darcy who, in Pride and Prejudice, published just two years earlier, was reported to have an income of similar proportions.

The early years of Norwich Union were an almost unqualified success. Not only did the business grow at a great rate, but its profitability was such that the policyholders (as owners) enjoyed significant financial benefits. The point about mutuality was that it provided the potential for either risk or reward. The members (i.e. the insured) were entitled to the whole of any distributable profit, but were liable for any losses. Perhaps the nearest modern parallel to this was Lloyds membership, at least in terms of the unlimited nature of personal liability. During the 1990s over 4 per cent of Lloyd's 'names', each of whom had held significant personal assets, were declared bankrupt after a series of disastrous under-writing results. No such disasters were experienced by the early policyholders of Norwich Union. Originally policies were established on a septennial basis, allowing an adequate term to review the results before the first bonus was declared. To encourage payment, a discount of one year's premium was offered to those who paid for seven years of cover at the outset. At the end of the first seven years, in 1804, conservative underwriting and a modest claims experience meant that each policyholder received the return of as much as 75 per cent of all the premiums they had paid in the preceding seven years.

Bignold had established a network of agents, mainly in Norfolk and Suffolk, and nearly three quarters of the business thus far emanated from those two counties. The success achieved to that point encouraged him to seek geographical expansion, and in a reprise of his experience with Norwich General this led him into conflict with the directors, culminating in the confrontation in April 1805 when he threatened them physically.

The unease of the directors over Bignold's ambitious plans was manifest at the Annual General Meeting in March of that year. A request by one of the trustees for access to the Society's books was refused by Bignold, and the directors determined to dismiss him.

It was at the next meeting, the following week, that Bignold threatened the directors with tongs and pistol. The directors realised that the only means of engineering Bignold's dismissal was through the medium of a Special General Meeting as laid down in the Deed of Settlement. At this meeting the directors maintained that, as his remuneration was based solely on premium he was set on expansion regardless of profit and this would inevitably end in tears. Bignold pointed to the highly successful record thus far as evidence of the effectiveness of his methods.

The real issue of substance however was the extent to which Bignold could follow his own devices and desires in managing the organisation regardless of the Board's views. Bignold was so successful in obtaining the support of the policyholder members, delighted with their 75 per cent bonus, that he won the vote on the issue of his continued employment hands down, getting support from over 80 per cent of those voting, thus frustrating the directors. Further he was able to obtain support for an amendment to the Deed of Settlement changing the role and constitution of the Board. So long as he enjoyed the confidence of the policyholder members he could do pretty well as he liked. The obvious candidates for the Board, the wealthy men of the city, were already engaged on the board of the Norwich General he had left, and this meant that membership of the Norwich Union Board could be offered to those of lower professional status, likely to be more amenable to indulging Bignold's ambitions.

This highlighted another aspect of mutuality – it made it more difficult to bring about change at the top. Today we sometimes see situations in which a chief executive is dismissed from a company very soon after disaffection becomes apparent. This can be done because it is the share, rather than the shareholder, which carries the right to vote. Shares are held in different numbers – the largest shareholders are institutions such as pension schemes, banks and insurance companies. The investment managers of such institutions have enormous block voting powers. Professional investors will carry out a continuous and robust scrutiny of the companies in which they invest and a relatively small number of such investors reaching a similar conclusion can attain a majority in favour of a particular course of action. Compare this with the situation in a mutual insurance company. While each policyholder is a part owner, he only has one vote. Ownership is therefore much more widely spread – there are no 'block votes'. Organising a revolution is much harder; many more people have to be canvassed and persuaded and they are less likely to be well informed of the issues. This aspect of mutuality was to be a frustration to the directors for many years in their attempts both to manage, and finally to dismiss, Bignold.

With his position intact Bignold began to use his power to further the interests of his family. With his pistol-packing son, (John Cocksedge Bignold) he formed a bank to handle the Norwich Union's business. Another son, Thomas, a solicitor, took over the legal work of the Society.

Freed from the constraint of effective management by the Board he continued his policy of expansion and out, first, went the bar on writing policies to cover specialist risks. Then that on insuring London property, and the £3,000 limit of cover was increased to £10,000. Insurance was certainly still not a mature market and there was a large amount of business to be written. His marketing skills and the large network of agencies he built up enabled him to begin seriously to challenge the domination of the London companies. As the business grew, so did the competition. While rates and limitations of cover were both elements of that competition, growth mainly resulted from the continued appointment of new agents, and something approaching national coverage had been achieved by 1811. At the time of the crisis in 1818 there were in excess of 500 agents, remunerated by a commission of 10 per cent on the premiums they generated by selling policies. With the need to compete on premium reduced by the operation of bonus refunds (strenuously promoted by Bignold in the press), the growth of the agency base and the image of the institution enhanced by the appointment of distinguished (though commercially naive) Trustees, Norwich Union grew its market share very fast. Bignold continued to expand his family connection with the business too, and in 1814 another son, Samuel, was appointed as Joint Secretary.

Initially, the relaxation of some underwriting requirements did not seem to affect profitability too greatly; bonuses continued to be in the order of 50 per cent, but as the economic climate deteriorated, especially after the Napoleonic Wars, the incidence of claims began to climb. Norwich Union responded by the establishment of local committees whose purpose was both to produce additional business and administer claims procedures – these were the forerunner of the branch network of later years. Declining economic times also led to concerns relating to 'moral hazard', characterised by a policyholder 'padding' a claim to overstate the loss or even committing outright arson. These issues were, to some extent, the cause of the conditions that led to the 1818 falling out.

Even though by 1815 Norwich Union had successfully secured the convictions of four insured members for making fraudulent claims, they continued to increase. Bignold had recently removed himself to London, leaving his son Samuel in charge at Norwich. His sons had, according to his great great grandson, Sir Robert, 'come to regard his presence in Norwich as tiresome'. Once in London his approach to claimants became arbitrary and damaging to the company's reputation. So too were his manoeuvres in the courts for the recovery of sums owed. The Society began to acquire a reputation for seeking to avoid claims, and doubts began to be held about its financial stability. Bignold, in 1817, compounded this by a contemptuous performance when summoned before a Select Committee of the House of Commons reviewing the use of Extents in Aid, a mechanism for pursuing debtors, frequently to bankruptcy, by claiming that the money owed was required to settle a debt to the Crown, for example in respect of duty payable on policies issued. Norwich Union was not alone in abusing this statutory power to recover debts, but was a particular exponent of the practice. This mechanism enabled the insurer, as creditor, to leapfrog all others to whom the debtor owed money, and it was one of Bignold's abuses of the mechanism which had brought about the establishment of the Select Committee, chaired by William Smith, a Norwich MP politically opposed to the Tories who by then dominated the Norwich Union Board.

In respect of the claims, it is probable that Bignold's instinct that many were either exorbitant or simply fabricated as a result of deliberately started fires was correct. But other companies paid out and tightened both their underwriting and their claims procedures. Bignold not only didn't pay, but didn't pay with an arrogance which caused great anger. As Sir Robert Bignold put it 'he seems simply to have dug in his toes and refused flatly to pay what appeared to be bona fide claims'.

Several examples were subsequently cited. In one, a claim by a Mr Deal, a claim assessed at £50, Thomas Bignold stone-walled with a will. First he told Deal that he was not insured, then that his claim was excessive. At a third meeting Deal was told that the Board had agreed to pay £35, but that as some of the goods might be recovered, Bignold would only pay him £25. In another a Mr Stubbs, after mutually agreed arbitration, was awarded £2,931. When the money was not paid, Stubbs took action in the High Court for payment by

Bignold. Reportedly Bignold promptly went to Norwich and when Stubbs followed him there, just as promptly returned to London again, travelling in the more expensive inside seats on the coach, while the pursuing Stubbs sat on the cheaper outside seats of the same vehicle. According to a circular letter prepared by disaffected claimants, Bignold was then 'taken in execution by the Sheriff of Surrey's warrant, kept in custody, and compelled to find the means of satisfying the award'.

Bignold had involved the Norwich Union in an expensive series of legal actions, all without the knowledge and consent of the Board, and the nature of them, and his behaviour, started to do serious reputational damage to Norwich Union in London. The Board, or so they claimed, only became aware of what was happening when one particular case, of a Mr Waldegrave, an insured driven to bankruptcy, attracted great public interest. Counsel was scathing about Mr Bignold's 'ungracious defence' which partially depended on an unsupported assertion of fraud on the part of the insured, which the jury didn't swallow. On investigating, the directors discovered that there were other matters before the courts as well. They said (statement submitted by the Board at the Special General Meeting on 9th November 1818) that Bignold had been 'continually treating clients with indignity and insult, and that his general conduct....was arbitrary and improper'.

As the discontent grew, no doubt to the satisfaction of his competitors, the feeling against Bignold hardened. At the Annual General Meeting the confidence members might have continued to repose in Bignold was eroded by the disclosure of the scale of recent losses. These were largely attributed to fraud, and were seen as an early warning that from being a means of obtaining cheap insurance mutuality might suddenly prove costly.

On July 23rd 1818, a meeting was held in London, at The George & Vulture Tavern, organised by 'The Suffering

Members from Insurance with the Norwich Union'. There is a possibility that competitors encouraged the meeting, following which a leaflet was produced and widely distributed door to door, addressed to 'The Proprietor of this House'.

A copy of this early piece of unsolicited mail remains in the Aviva archives – it is an extraordinary, if very one-sided diatribe. Apart from the account, referred to above, of the claim by Mr Stubbs, it attacked the Society in very flowery terms, and on a number of fronts. It declared that the trustees (those 'names of distinction' supposed to add credibility to the Society), 'disclaimed any knowledge or interest in it'. Earl Craven was claimed, for example, to have agreed to lend his name only when requested to do so by the 'Dancing Master to his family'. Nor was the Earl Craven the only trustee to have little or no involvement with the company. The Earl of Rosebery declined, when later approached by John Patteson (q.v.), in his capacity as President of Norwich Union, to become involved in the proposed dismissal of Thomas Bignold. He said that he 'meant only to be one of the patrons of the Society', and that 'it was never his intention to interfere in the smallest degree with any of its concerns'. Bignold's response to the mutterings about these 'names of distinction' was totally in character. 'Is it supposed', he asked, 'that His Grace the Duke of Argyll has a desk and stool at the office in Norwich or London, and keeps the Cash Book?' The dancing master who importuned Craven was himself a director, Francis Noverre. The other directors were also named, for the most part farmers and small businessmen.

The meeting established a committee to investigate unsettled claims, and concluded that 'This heterogeneous co-partnership' was under the sole management of Thomas and Samuel Bignold, as it was 'quite ridiculous to think that the directors (who are mostly Farmers and Tradesmen) have anything to do with the concern other than to act as the automatons of these private bankers'. The directors responded to this affront promptly, arranging a meeting in

London themselves, which took place just four days later, and which also established a committee of London members to investigate the situation.

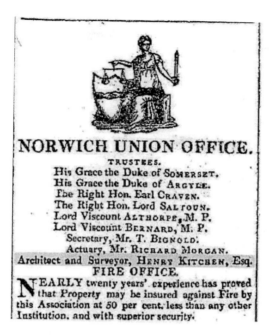

Liverpool Mercury **advertisement of 1815 highlighting the distinguished trustees**

Characteristically, Bignold cooperated with neither, but the committee established at the meeting called by the directors reported back, having received support and help from his son, Samuel. The report was discussed at a further meeting, held at The London Tavern in Bishopsgate on 25th September. It was of enough public interest to justify a lengthy report in *The Times* of the following day. This report described the attendance as 'very numerous and very respectable' and the appointed chairman, Mr Bensley, as accepting the responsibility very unwillingly. It is clear as one reads the report that there was something of an ugly mood, and Bensley obviously anticipated trouble, saying that it was under the protection of his colleagues that he 'should be able to preserve order'. The report, described as 'very long' was read and examined a number of factors, ranging from the financial standing of both Fire and Life Societies, through the history of rejected claims to the constitution of the Society and the behaviour of Thomas Bignold. The financial picture appeared reasonably satisfactory, and there was some evidence that a number of claims had been dealt with appropriately, but the committee expressed several concerns; the Deeds of Settlement 'had very great defects', the securities held in Bignold's own name should be transferred to the ownership of the Societies, and remedial action was needed so that Norwich Union could 'bid fair to raise itself to the propriety which its warmest supporters could wish'.

The report commented very favourably on the behaviour of his sons, Samuel and Thomas (Junior) but was highly critical of Thomas Bignold and concluded that 'the immediate retirement of that gentleman from his office of Secretary was indispensably necessary for the future welfare of the institution'.

At this, one member of the audience, Mr Barry, a barrister, complained that Thomas was being condemned unheard, and another said that, as he was present, he should seek to defend himself 'if he could'. The section of the report relating to the alleged failings of Thomas was read again, 'to loud applause'. Barry spoke again... 'it was the right of every Englishman to be heard' and the report should only be adopted if the section criticising Bignold was dropped, as the progress of the Society was due to his zeal. This view attracted a less enthusiastic reception but, nonetheless, 'partial applause'. A member of the committee then stepped in. The recommendations of the committee were justified and they had hoped that Bignold would fall on his sword before the meeting; his zeal was not in question but his judgement was. He added, to great applause, that Bignold had to go for the sake of the Society.

Bignold rose to defend himself. The complaints against him were the work of rivals, the enemies of the Society were seeking to deprive it of his skills. Isolated other members rose to defend him, but struggled to make themselves heard in a clearly hostile audience and the proposed amendment, to accept the report with the exception of the criticism of Bignold was rejected by a large majority and the original, complete, form adopted.

At a meeting in November, the directors gave their response in a full statement which confirmed their acknowledgement that Bignold had failed to disclose many details to them, and that his behaviour had been unsatisfactory and had led to serious damage to the Society's reputation. More importantly it asserted that the London end of the business must, in future, be run differently. It regretted that Bignold had failed to 'comport himself with civility and respect' towards the committee, and passed a resolution that he should be dismissed. The resolution was passed unanimously by the meeting, estimates of the number of insured members attending varying between four and five hundred, and the vote being taken to shouts of 'all, all' as hands were raised to vote for his dismissal.

The language of the report is interesting. While it is quite clear that they found Bignold's behaviour reprehensible and no longer to be tolerated, one senses a degree of regret on the part of the Board. They acknowledged the huge contribution he had made in the early stages of the Society and sought to sugar the pill with a suggestion that he should be rewarded with an income for life. The final paragraph encapsulates this, expressing the hope that the recollection of his past services would mitigate the degree of censure.

The London committee asked for a General Meeting to agree the most effective way of dismissing Bignold. They also flexed their muscles and sought to take over control of the Society, a move scotched by the Board's decision not to write new insurances in London. Instead the Board itself called a General Meeting to obtain approval for his dismissal.

Whether the reference in the report to Bignold's achievements was inserted at the behest of his sons is not known, but if it was intended to incline Bignold to go with good grace it failed, miserably. He responded with anger, making personal attacks on his sons.

Following the meeting, which had been held at the George and Vulture Tavern, Bignold had promptly published a rejection of all criticism in a leaflet snappily entitled:

'An Exposure of the unjustifiable
proceedings and Unworthy Motives of
Mr. Thorpe and others, holding the late
meetings at the George and Vulture Tavern;
refuting the Fabricated Reports which they
have lately issued and shewing
THE EFFECT WHICH CALUMNY SO
MALIGNANT AND PREMEDITATED IS
LIKELY TO PRODUCE ON THE
SOCIETY.'

As might be expected, his reaction to calls for his dismissal was simply to ignore them and carry on. Matters moved slowly, the directors and his sons still hoped for a relatively amicable parting of the ways, but there was little chance of that. Bignold even started yet another insurance company to compete with Norwich Union and to add to the confusion named it the National Union. Eventually the Board obtained enough support for his dismissal from both the Fire and Life companies, but he delayed them again by recourse to the courts. It wasn't until 1822 that his dismissal from the Norwich Union Fire Society was achieved, and he still laid claim to the Secretaryship of the increasingly important Life Society. It took until 1825 for him to agree that Samuel should be the Secretary of that company also. By that time he had been imprisoned for debt and declared a bankrupt, as

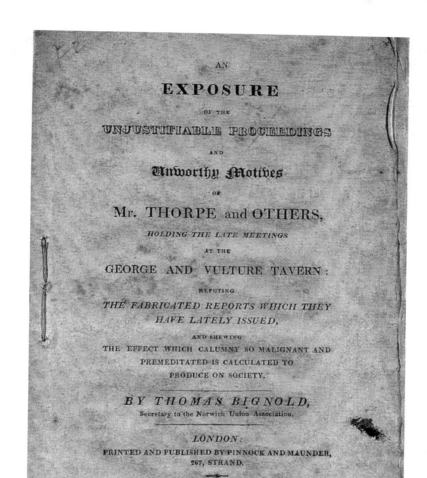

AN

EXPOSURE

OF THE

UNJUSTIFIABLE PROCEEDINGS

AND

Unworthy Motives

OF

Mr. THORPE and OTHERS,

HOLDING THE LATE MEETINGS

AT THE

GEORGE AND VULTURE TAVERN:

REFUTING

*THE FABRICATED REPORTS WHICH THEY
HAVE LATELY ISSUED,*

AND SHEWING

THE EFFECT WHICH CALUMNY SO MALIGNANT AND
PREMEDITATED IS CALCULATED TO
PRODUCE ON SOCIETY.

BY THOMAS BIGNOLD,
Secretary to the Norwich Union Association.

LONDON:
PRINTED AND PUBLISHED BY PINNOCK AND MAUNDER,
267, STRAND.

1818.

reported in the *London Gazette* of 1st November 1823, in which he was described simply as 'a dealer in boots and shoes'. He was still contesting the proceedings eleven years later.

When Bignold fell, he fell a long way, and it was not a soft landing. The journey from the support of the huge majority of policyholder members at the meeting in 1805 to the unanimous vote for his dismissal thirteen years later must have been uncomfortable enough, but it was followed by indignity after indignity. Sixteen months in a debtor's prison, adjudged bankrupt in 1823, and in 1827 he even had to go to court to recover his dirty laundry from the pawnbroker to whom his washerwoman had hocked it. In the latter incident the pawnbroker managed to get in a blow below the belt when, from the box, he contrasted his own 'established character' with the public perception of Bignold. Accustomed as he must by then have become to the metaphorical washing of his dirty linen in public this literal example must have been particularly demeaning. At least he got his washing back, if not his dignity.

Bignold was not, perhaps, an entirely honourable man either in his business or his private life. *The Morning Post* of 21st October 1820 reported an interesting case heard in the High Court the previous day. Thomas had taken an action against his son, John Cocksedge, to recover £3,000 owed under a bond executed by his son. However, it transpired that all was not as it might have appeared. Thomas, the court was told by his son's counsel, had wanted his son to marry a Miss Crowe and it had been arranged between him and the bride's father that the latter would settle £4,000 on his daughter, and Bignold £3,000 on Thomas. These settlements were executed after the marriage, which took place in April 1816. Thomas had, without the knowledge of either his daughter-in-law or her father, arranged to recoup the sum by inducing his son to give him a bond for the same amount, thereby defrauding Mr Crowe and his daughter. At one point the judge intervened to say that as both Bignolds, senior and junior, had been parties to the fraud the jury's decision, that the son must repay the father, was correct.

What this incident did to the marital relationship one cannot tell, and sadly the former Miss Crowe died the year after the case and only five years after her marriage. Her husband died just two years later at the age of thirty-seven. They left two daughters, born in 1817 and 1819 who died at the ages of eighteen and thirteen respectively. The father of the bride, described as 'a gentleman' was John Crowe – the same John Crowe was Chairman of Norwich Union at the time of the dismissal proceedings against Thomas Bignold in 1818. Family gatherings during the brief marriage must have been interesting affairs.

Neither was Bignold renowned for his diplomacy. One well-documented story tells how, when he bragged that he could offer insurance against anything, he was asked whether he could insure his questioner against being bitten by a mad dog. 'No', Bignold is said to have replied, 'because, if you were to be bitten by a dog, I should not consider that the dog was mad!'

He had, with his son John Cocksedge, founded a bank in the halcyon days, and it would seem that he may not have been imbued with a great charitable spirit either, at least if a rather sad appeal in the local press is anything to go by. The following appeared on March 8th 1806:

> Mrs White is impelled, by the misfortunes of her Husband, to obtrude herself on the public attention on behalf of her FIFTEEN CHILDREN now with her, the sixteenth being in the service of his country as a Midshipman, and was so wounded in the battle of Trafalgar, when he had been but a few weeks in the service, that he will be lame for life; she has used every effort for the maintenance of her family, but now that the beds are about to be torn from under her children, and sold with every other article of furniture, she and they must be without money, without food, without raiment, and in want of every other convenience, unless the honest and the generous will compassionate (sic) and relieve their distress.

> Subscriptions will be received at all the banks in Norwich, except by Mr Bignold's, and by Mrs White herself at 43 London-lane Norwich, by whom they will be most gratefully acknowledged.

After all the years of indignity and poverty Thomas eventually reached an uneasy compromise; there was some limited sort of rapprochement with his sons and in a final piece of horse-trading, he received a cash sum and an annuity on returning to Norwich Union a number of securities which had been placed in his name before the 1818 dispute. In 1825 he returned to Kent. Four years later his health began to suffer after he broke a leg falling from a horse he had just bought, but he lived until 1835, when, still in Kent, he died from apoplexy. Samuel arranged for his body to be brought back to Norwich for burial.

Thomas Bignold was certainly a slippery customer, arrogant, arbitrary, manipulative, evasive and not wholly honest. But he was also visionary, persistent, an indefatigable worker and an exceptionally high achiever. He was not the sort of man it would have been easy to manage and he must have been very frustrating to deal with. But one can only admire his energy, his ambition and his commitment, even while wondering whether, in later years, he crossed the narrow line between extreme eccentricity and insanity. And that perhaps would not be surprising given both how far he fell and his own character. It is difficult not to feel a little sympathetic towards a man who achieved so much but ended up not just broke, but reviled and rejected by those who had benefited from his imagination and energy.

Postscript

Norwich Union suffered significantly in the years of the dispute and afterwards. It was Bignold's son, Samuel, who negotiated a merger with Norwich General, the company his father had so unceremoniously ditched to set up Norwich

Union in 1821, a move that stabilised Norwich Union Fire, which became a joint stock company.

Norwich Union continued to grow, though not without some pains, both organically and by acquisition. One company they acquired was The Amicable Society, whose claim to be the oldest insurer in the world operating on actuarial principles, founded in 1706, did not prevent their need for a bigger parent, given the losses they incurred as a result of the South Sea Bubble. Ironically, the author's great great grandfather was a director of the Amicable at the time and in his diary fulminated at the supine nature of his fellow Board members in giving such a prize to Norwich Union. The entry when he visited the office for the last time and found Samuel Bignold in possession is almost sulphurous.

Norwich Union grew not just in Britain, but overseas as well, especially in the colonies and the United States. Mutuality had been necessarily discarded by the Fire Society on the merger with Norwich General, but the Life Society, which in 1924 purchased the Fire Society in a deal that required them to tie up almost a quarter of their investment capital, retained its mutuality until as late as 1997, when in its bicentenary year it floated on the Stock Market. It didn't remain independent long – merger with the CGU (the company formed by the merger of the Commercial Union and General Accident companies) coming in 2000. Two years later the Group was re-branded Aviva, although the Norwich Union brand continued to be used in the United Kingdom until 2009. Thomas Bignold would have expected nothing less.

Sources:
Material in the Aviva Group Archive
Norwich Mercury Archives at the Heritage Centre at Norwich Millennium Library
The Times Digital Archive

'Banking and Insurance', Roger Ryan, in *Norwich since 1550*, see bibliography.

A History of the Norwich Union Fire & Life Societies from 1797 to 1914, Roger Ryan (PhD Thesis submitted to the university of East Anglia in October 1983)

Five Generations of the Bignold Family 1761-1947 and their connection with the Norwich Union, Sir Robert Bignold, see bibliography.

John Jarrold II (1773-1852)
Retailer, Farmer, Printer, Publisher, and man of social conscience.

John Jarrold started in a modest way at Woodbridge in Suffolk. Here fortune speedily smiled upon him, or perhaps we should say that his methods were such as to compel the compliance of that fickle goddess.

A Descriptive Account of Norwich, c 1890

John Jarrold II (JJ) was the only son of John Jarrold, a Suffolk draper. He had four older sisters. John (senior) had been born just over the Essex border, in Manningtree, a descendant of several Essex generations of an originally Huguenot family. John (senior) was a meticulous and organised man, who, while apprenticed in Woodbridge, wrote for himself a set of rules governing his life, and particularly his business life. These rules included the prompt payment of debt, honesty, never to borrow or to lend, to keep proper accounts, to treat every customer equally, not to over-egg his goods and to have regard for the Christian religion – a veritable manifesto for self-improvement.

The existence of these rules was, perhaps, the only direct influence he could have on his son, as he died at the age of 30, when JJ was only two, leaving a business in Woodbridge which JJ's mother ran for two years before moving with JJ to Norwich (where she had family) leaving her daughters in Suffolk. A clue to the background of this unusual arrangement may be found in the notes of a meeting of the Congregational Church in Woodbridge and subsequent correspondence. Following a meeting on July 14th 1785, the notes disclose that 'it was agreed by the brethren that Elizabeth Jarrold, one of our Members, having in many ways acted contrary to her Christian profession, and particularly to the disgrace of it by her spirit of conduct towards her own daughters, should now...be set aside from communion with us'.

A letter was sent to JJ's mother confirming her excommunication, brought about particularly by 'the conduct you have assumed to your own daughters, inconsistant (sic) with humanity and Christianity – this has brought public reproach upon your profession [presumably of faith] and character'. The letter went on to say that she was excommunicated until such time as she could demonstrate 'a proper sence (sic) of her past misconduct' and the will 'to exercise a better temper'. The nature of the difficulties in the relationship between mother and daughters is unclear but, when Mrs Jarrold died, in December the same year, they were clearly unresolved as one of the church deacons wrote to her attorney in Norwich saying 'I have often indulged the hope that some future period might witness Mrs Jarrold's conviction of her error and mutual reconciliation between herself and her children but the all-wise disposer of events has otherwise decided'. The attorney was a Mr Cooper, and the deacon continued, 'It will no doubt be a source of satisfaction to the children and their Friends (guardians) that you are interested (involved) in the management of their mother's affairs'. The deacon could hardly have been more wrong.

JJ at 12 was, as the sole male member of the family, left with responsibility not just for himself, but for his sisters too. JJ while nominally in the care of Cranwell Coates of Gainsborough, his maternal grandfather, was actually taken in by one of the two executors of his mother's estate, the other, the attorney Cooper, taking responsibility for the investment of the assets in government securities. One executor proved a rather better steward than the other.

The assets were significant. On attaining the age of twenty-one, John (senior) had inherited £1,000 (worth today about £110,000) which he had put to good use, purchasing business premises in the Market Place in Woodbridge. By 1785, the family fortune amounted to some £13,000, close to £1,500,000 in 2012 values. The investment of some of the funds was entrusted to Cooper. Unfortunately he proved unworthy of the trust, embezzling the whole sum, confirming the worst fears of JJ's sisters whose correspondence with their brother was full of anxieties about Cooper's tardiness in paying them what was due. Regaining as much as possible of the capital, took nearly thirty years.

Fortunately JJ was luckier with his mother's other executor, John Bidwell, who gave him a home and then, when JJ was 14, arranged for him to be apprenticed to a grocer in Stalham, one Obadiah Silcock, who described him as 'sober, honest and industrious and a responsible person in whom confidence could be placed'. JJ had obviously made a good impression, demonstrating a particular skill in calculation and accounts. JJ still had access to a small amount of money, and, with encouragement from Silcock, invested this in a partnership with Bidwell as a shawl-maker. He was still just an apprentice, but clearly he was one with ambition and entrepreneurial instincts.

When it became clear that the lawyer, Cooper, had spent the money he was to have invested for the Jarrold children, Silcock arranged for JJ to be advised by a Suffolk lawyer from Halesworth, John Lomas Cufaude. Members of JJ's family had already advised against taking the matter to the Court of Chancery; a cousin wrote to him 'You talk of putting your affairs into Chancery – desist by all means'. Even 50 years before Dickens exposed its frailties in *Bleak House* the Court of Chancery was well known as a source of delay and as much an impoverishment to claimants as it was an enrichment to the lawyers. Cufaude's advice to JJ enabled him, over the long term, to recover the greater part of the capital.

This recovery was not without its moments of drama. In a letter to JJ dated 19th August 1796, Cufaude described the result when, on his advice, the bailiff was instructed to apprehend Cooper: 'the bailiff informed me that he took him on the Thorp (sic) road as he was going to Oby about half past ten at night'. It was so dark, reported the bailiff, that he nearly missed Cooper who was 'sat huddled up with a sailor's coat or jacket, and his boy driving'. The bailiff had to grab the reins and seize Cooper himself' to secure him'.

Cooper suggested guarantors as additional security for a bond he proposed to assign to JJ to cover his liabilities, but Cufaude was cautious – his investigation into the proposed sureties was not encouraging. He reported to JJ in early November that one was 'not a safe man', having been bankrupt. The other was 'a very expensive man, keeping women in the house'. Yet a third was suggested, but it transpired that he was a financial dependant of Cooper, and he would not therefore offer any additional security if Cooper failed.

On Cufaude's advice, JJ calculated, in meticulous detail, the extent of Cooper's debt, including interest. The calculation sheets together with the correspondence between JJ and Cufaude can still be examined at the Norfolk Record Office. Eventually Cooper agreed to make repayment over time.

Meanwhile JJ had reached the end of his apprenticeship and his solvency improved as Cooper's repayments began, and he sold property in Yorkshire, inherited from his mother's family. He decided to use this money to set up as a grocer back in Woodbridge. In October 1797 a handbill was produced, describing him as a grocer and draper, and explaining that he had taken over the premises of a Mr Tayler and re-stocked 'in all departments', and 'respectfully solicits the favour of former customers, and of the public....assuring them of his determination to sell every article on the lowest terms'. He took the opportunity the handbill offered to promote a Sale of the old stock 'at prime cost and under'. Retailing was in his blood. So too was the prompt payment of bills, as recommended by his late father. Being able to pay cash up front endeared him to wholesalers who were more inclined to discount to him than to other retailers.

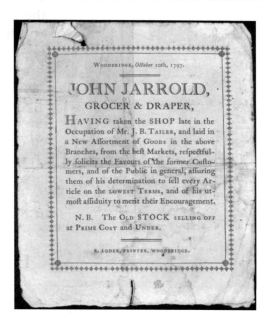

In 1800 JJ married Hannah Hill, of Bungay. While apprenticed to Obadiah Silcock he had lived with the family, and it is probable that Hannah Hills was a relation of theirs. Their first son, John James Jarrold, was born in 1803, and their second, Samuel, in 1805. Three more sons and a daughter followed, but of these only two of the sons – William Pightling (1807) and Thomas (1812) survived to adulthood.

In the meantime, JJ had shown that, while retailing may have been in his blood, he was quite prepared to extend his interests. Competition in the retail trade was fierce, and JJ was flexible; if other opportunities looked promising then he was quite happy to invest. His first foray outside shopkeeping was in farming. He purchased a farm of 114 acres at Dallinghoo, near Woodbridge. Initially it proved a shrewd move as food prices rose during the Napoleonic wars. JJ managed the farm with the attention to detail that had characterised his calculation of Cooper's debt. He kept an expenses book, recording a payment of the sum of 2/6d for the killing of rats, £1.1s.6d for two days threshing, and a payment to the 'Cow Doctor' of £1.17s.0d. He was as careful in recording the income, with the type of crop and the yield recorded on a field by field basis. With rising prices and strict budgeting the profits were good. When the war ended in 1815 however, as wages rose and food prices fell, farming ceased to be as profitable. But apart from being a home with room for his wife and growing family, the farm also played an important part in the Jarrold's story, as the first base for what was to become a core element in the company's success for generations, printing and publishing.

Farming was not the only alternative business to attract JJ's interest, he also became part owner of a trading brig, thus completing a commercial trinity of production (from the farm), distribution and retail. Neither was it just business which occupied his mind during those years. His father's determination, expressed in his commonplace book, to have regard for the Christian religion, burned as fiercely in JJ. Like his father he had a strong faith and he became an active and evangelical member of the Congregational Church. In nearby Wickham Market, the church met in the house of one of its members. Nonconformism was anathema to the local vicar and also, it appears, to some of the local population. Around 1810 worship was regularly interrupted by the sounds of the mob, equipped with trumpets, gongs and drums. Worse was to follow, as the mob threw things at the preacher, including 'hollowed out turnips filled with the most detestable filth'. JJ was involved in taking these matters to court. The magistrates were unmoved, and the matter had to be taken to the King's Bench, partly at JJ's own expense, before the culprits were fined, and bound over to keep the peace. Meanwhile he had his own home registered as a place of worship to accommodate the congregation.

Soon after this, in 1812, JJ sponsored Benjamin Smith, the husband of his sister-in-law, by purchasing premises for him in Woodbridge. Smith was a printer and three years later JJ entered into a partnership with him, the first Jarrold foray into printing and publishing. Smith decided to leave the trade in 1821, so JJ was left with the printing machinery. He moved this into a barn at his farm at Dallinghoo and continued to act as a publisher under the name of Jarrold & Son when his eldest son, John James, was eighteen.

Access to the facility for printing and publishing enabled JJ to give public expression to his quite radical views. A series of pamphlets written by him and promoting social change emerged from the Jarrold presses. He was particularly concerned at the growing trend to impoverishment in the labouring classes. He even invited the support of the famous anti-slavery campaigner Thomas Clarkson in his campaign by sending him, in 1824, a copy of one pamphlet drawing attention to the 'increasing pauperism' in 'this once happy country'. Clarkson was later only one of a number of such men of conscience to be entertained by JJ in Norwich. There can be little doubt of the sincerity of his concern for social justice – seeking improvement was a lifelong mission. Even as late as 1851 he published, under the pseudonym 'a Patriot', a pamphlet entitled 'Miscellaneous thoughts concerning the weal and woe of England'. He was not the only Jarrold to publish such tracts, which continued in the next generation. By 1873 Jarrold's *Household Tracts for the People* had a circulation of over four million, according to the City Treasurer in a paper read that year to the Social Science Congress in Norwich.

But JJ wasn't just a writer of improving tracts, he was a generous benefactor to a number of good causes, admitting that he gave away a larger sum each year in such charitable donations than he paid to any of his sons. In particular he was, like others in this book, a supporter of the City Mission in Norwich, providing active help to encourage its missionaries which continued in his retirement.

In contrast to his relationship with his younger sons (as we shall see later) JJ clearly had a real rapport with John James and, in 1823, the two of them moved to Norwich, a city JJ knew well, the nearest major commercial centre, where they set up as booksellers. Tradition has it that they arrived with £7,000 in cash – value in 2012 well over £500,000 – and, thus equipped were soon able to acquire premises, not far from the location of Jarrold's store today.

His other sons followed, Samuel to work in the shop, William Pightling to be apprenticed to a draper, and Thomas, having spent some time in London, joined the business in 1830. JJ's rapport with John James was not replicated with his other sons, particularly Samuel, of whom he later wrote... 'as to Samuel...it would have been far better had he gone from home as an apprentice or journeyman under an intelligent Master for improvement and to be accustomed to a proper degree of subordination, learning the art of obedience, and not to lord it over others, or think more highly of himself than he ought to think'.

Propinquity didn't make matters easier. Fortunately John James was an effective buffer between his father and his brothers. Indeed, it appears that JJ would only communicate with his younger sons through the medium of their brother, whose advocacy on his brothers' behalf persuaded his father to re-name the business by turning 'Jarrold & Son' into 'Jarrold & Sons'. The sons, perhaps naturally, believed that this meant that they were full partners in the business. It seems clear though that JJ regarded this change simply as window-dressing, and that the control of the business was his, with some input from his eldest son. His attitude seems clear in a letter he wrote to Samuel many years later (1845) that, in 1823, 'I and my elder son came to Norwich and guided by our all wise benevolent providence, I with his personal assistance commenced a Bookselling, Printing and Binding Business. God in his gracious providence, from a small business has continued to enlarge the Business and to grant prosperity'. In other words, success was attributable to the efforts of JJ, the grace of God and an occasional input from John James – and not at all as a result of the efforts of the three younger sons.

JJ's wife, Hannah, died in 1840 and just three years later John James died suddenly, at the age of forty, from rheumatic fever. The channel between father and younger sons died

63

with him. By this time the company had expanded drama-tically, JJ having taken every opportunity to purchase property adjacent to their original site, but still the arguments had not abated. While the business continued to prosper, the atmo-sphere deteriorated apace. Communication, hitherto carried out via John James, was so strained that it was carried out in writing, even when the parties saw each other daily. The differences between the generations must have been obvious to the staff. On one occasion Samuel countermanded an instruction given by JJ for an alteration to the premises, requiring the previous position to be restored. JJ's relation-ships with his three younger sons make a parallel with those of Bignold and his sons more than forty years earlier - inter-generational disagreement, with the younger generation wanting to develop the business in their own way, and the father resenting his young biting the hand that he felt had fed them. But at least with the Jarrolds, the infighting was relatively private rather than being played out in the public arena as with the Bignolds, and the company continued to enjoy a reputation as a fair and enlightened employer.

Perhaps surprisingly, given the disagreements, the business continued to prosper. In the field of publishing one of the success stories of this period was the publication of Ebenezer Brewer's *'A Guide to the Scientific Knowledge of Things Familiar'* a perennial worldwide seller of which nearly fifty editions were published in England alone in the next fifty years. More than 100,000 copies had been produced by Jarrold's by 1873. Thomas Jarrold is said to have declined to purchase the copyright of this book early on for a mere £50, but agreed to publish the book on a profit sharing basis. Such was its success that Jarrold subsequently refused an offer of £4,000 from Brewer for his share of future sales.

'Mr Jarrold retired from the partnership, leaving the business to his three surviving sons'. So at least it was written in *The House of Jarrolds,* published in 1924 by the company itself.

But this simple description is little more than the forerunner of the sort of bland statements issued today by political leaders after an empty summit. Everything sounds measured, thought through, and under control. The reality is different.

The disagreements between JJ and his sons were significant. They regarded themselves as partners; he saw them as managers, and not wholly competent ones at that. He was alarmed, particularly, by what he saw as their tendency to overstock, and forecast dire consequences if they had a free hand. He was disinclined to share information with them. They were not given access to the books, and he was prone to treat the company's assets as his own, withdrawing funds for personal investment in property. JJ's time-consuming interests outside the business must also have been an irritation to his sons who were engaged wholeheartedly in running it, especially given his treatment of them. Quite apart from the farm and his interests in other businesses, he was engaged in a range of other activities actively supporting the Temperance Movement (a cause he shared with his sons and Samuel in particular), the Anti-Slavery Movement and various Church Missions.

In 1845 JJ wrote to his sons: 'the receipt of yours of the 18th ultimo places you and me in a tangible business situation, enabling me and you to examine, and, when I consider you to be in error, arguing from erroneous principles, it is my duty to endeavour to set you right. Let me advise you to remember the duty you owe to your aged parent by the Laws of God, clearly revealed in the Bible, and by the laws of Mammon which if disobeyed would involve families and society in confusion.' He went on to refer both to his having had the perseverance, the industry and the frugality to succeed and to the need for careful consideration of potential partnerships given their consequences. It would seem that he still maintained that he was not in partnership with them.

JJ was inclined to spend time at Dallinghoo and it was on one of these occasions, in 1846, that the sons determined on decisive action to resolve the issue once and for all. The most fundamental aspect of the matter was the issue of partnership. They believed themselves to be legally in partnership with their father, he regarded the style of 'Jarrold & Sons' to be a sham, a device for enhancing their status without legal implication.

To resolve the confusion, the sons decided to enlist the help of a man respected by both sides, Jacob Tillett. Tillett was a formidable man of high reputation. A solicitor, a prominent Liberal and, later, with Thomas Jarrold, Jeremiah Colman and John Copeman, one of the founders of the *Norfolk News*, the forerunner of the *Eastern Daily Press*. Tillett was a campaigner against corruption; ironically his initial election to Parliament was overturned because of bribery by others acting in the capacity of agent, though without his knowledge. Later elected successfully, his own character was beyond question.

The sons made written submissions to Tillett and, in the absence of their father, passed over to him the account books. Surprisingly compliant, JJ wrote to his son Thomas on August 14th, expressing his 'full reliance on Mr Tillett's discriminating ability to understand the Business and his wish to decide impartially'. But he was concerned to establish the basis upon which Tillett was to express an opinion. He insisted that all three sons should come to the 'same agreement' and that Mr Tillett 'give me his written opinion and the leading ground of argument on which he relied'. And he was still not happy about Samuel who 'both by very candid language and writing has so impeached my character that it is requisite that I should be able to defend myself from any unfavourable impressions'. Nonetheless he signed off expressing the hope that 'by Mr Tillett's friendly aid we shall come to a right understanding and that harmony and good will again govern our mutual relationship'.

JJ also wrote to Tillett on a number of occasions explaining that he would be unwilling to respond in kind to any verbal remarks made by the brothers and insisting that Tillett should not arrive at a conclusion without a sight of JJ's written response to any such remark.

Tillett offered his conclusion in early September. It was to the effect that a partnership had existed since 1830, and that the sons were entitled to their share. In arriving at his decision he explained that it was based rather on fairness than legal considerations. He commented on the 'unusual' transactions between the partners and the lack of detail of financial withdrawals or of stocktaking. He acknowledged that this lack of evidence precluded him from arriving at a 'certain' conclusion, but expressed the belief that his decision was right 'in honour and justice'.

JJ responded promptly, pointing out that Thomas had been a minor in 1830 and asserting that his deceased son, John James, was entitled to be treated as a partner from the date of their joint arrival in Norwich, and he alone. He clearly also protested at some of the conclusions because Tillett responded, on September 16th, expressing regret that 'the clause in my award, stating that you had withdrawn money from the partnership has led to the impression that you had acted in a manner deserving censure'. This correspondence clearly represented the dying embers of JJ's flame of indignation for Tillett goes on to commend JJ for his acquiescence in the terms of the award, but JJ seems never to have wholly accepted the decision, persisting in referring to it as 'an opinion'. Given Tillett's own admission that he had reached his conclusion more on the grounds of equity than law, this seems a reasonable enough view. In a further letter JJ could not forbear, one more time, from reminding Tillett that his sons 'derive all their wealth from me', and thanking 'Divine providence for giving me enterprise to make another attempt to better my circumstances and to provide employment for my sons'.

JJ then retired to live in Coltishall, where he continued to be engaged in 'good works' and to attend worship in the chapel, where his failing hearing was supplemented by an arrangement of wires to his pew terminating in a 'cup' to be applied to his ear. He died in 1852.

Jarrolds Store on its present site in about 1909

JJ was in many ways a remarkable man. His character must have been forged early when, left an orphan, he had to come to grips first with the estrangement of his sisters from their mother and later their financial needs, and then with the business and the prolonged dispute with Cooper. Together these represented a serious challenge for someone so young. He was a man of courage, of responsibility, and of imagination, and an honest man. True he removed funds from the partnership to fund private investment, but then he didn't really accept that the partnership existed. It was, in his mind, still 'his' business. Even so, he sought to repay the

68

sums when the matter came to light. As a father he perhaps left something to be desired, but he had not had an example to follow and his childhood experience had been only of a parent estranged from her daughters - a lack of rapport may not have seemed unusual to him. He also lost his eldest and closest son and two of those who remained seem to have been much under the influence of the third, the rather fiery Samuel, with whom he did not get on.

He was a man committed to his faith, courageous and tenacious in his actions at Wickham Market. A man, too, of strong opinions and with a genuine concern for the social good. These strong opinions, when related to business, made him obstinate and difficult for his family to deal with. It should surely have been up to him to make more effort to break down the barriers between him and his sons; possibly he simply felt that they were both lacking in the respect for parents which in those days was seen as natural, and insufficiently appreciative of the fine opportunities he had created for them. His approach to John James, with whom he shared the initial development in Norwich, was very different.

In business he was a man of decision and intelligence, anticipating trends and moving adroitly to take advantage of a changing environment. Although in his later years it was printing that dominated the business he had put fingers into many commercial pies: shawl-making, farming and ship-owning as well as a range of retail businesses. He could, perhaps be best described as 'a portfolio entrepreneur'. The irony is that what became for many years the focus of the company was printing and publishing, an industry into which JJ entered into wholeheartedly, less as a deliberate strategy than as a means of using the plant available as a result of Benjamin Smith's decision to leave it.

Postscript

JJ's doubts about the competence of his sons (he once described them as 'useless') proved without foundation. They

69

mutually agreed and accepted fairly modest levels of remuneration and the business continued to prosper under their management. Technological development in the printing process was rapidly embraced by the brothers and the printing works rebuilt. Publishing also grew rapidly, especially in the field of educational books. By 1873 Thomas Hancock, the City Treasurer, was describing them as 'celebrated for the production of educational works'. In 1847 they opened a further publishing branch in London, reflecting their growing reputation in this field. Increased adult literacy also encouraged, in the spirit of the age, the publication of 'improving' pamphlets promoting domesticity, temperance and industriousness. These tracts were a particular enthusiasm of Samuel, especially in relation to temperance. Thomas proved particularly astute in his selection of which manuscripts to publish. As well as Brewer's Guide referred to earlier he had a spectacular success with Anna Sewell's 'Black Beauty'.

Aside from the core businesses of publishing and printing, the range of products sold in the store expanded into new areas. The brothers continued to run the business in apparent amity until Samuel died, in 1874, after catching a chill while distributing Temperance tracts. His death was followed two years later by that of the childless William Pightling Jarrold. The following year Thomas also died. His widow, and Samuel's, took up the challenge of finalising the production of Black Beauty.

With the death of Thomas, the responsibility for running the business moved on to yet another John, Samuel's son. John was simply salaried, his father having left the business to the two widows. John was but the stepson of Mrs Samuel who, favouring the two boys she had had with Samuel, appears to have taken against John with whom she was continually in conflict. Eventually John was able to buy the share owned by his aunt, Thomas's widow. Only two years later, in 1890 he died, at the age of 42, leaving his novice stepbrothers William and Herbert Jarrold to take over. They succeeded in continuing to grow the business, and in the early 1900s were responsible for the rebuilding of the store. This was probably overdue because, as the range of goods sold in the store grew wider, the premises, acquired piecemeal over the years, had become not only crowded, but confusing to customers. A surveyor had noted that the store was potentially dangerous in the event of fire. The transition to a department store was well timed, and areas were set aside for sports equipment, luggage and fancy goods as well as the traditional books and stationery. While printing and publishing were still key to the business, the store remained a visible flagship and additional services such as a café and a Reading Room were provided for the convenience of customers.

The twentieth century, with two world wars, was a period of great change for large and small companies, and Jarrold's was no exception; succeeding generations of Jarrolds have had to adopt a flexible approach to maintain the company's standing and profitability. In 1902, Jarrold & Sons became a Limited Liability Company though still in family hands. Herbert Jarrold's son, Herbert John, joined the company in 1928, the only member of his generation of the family to be involved in the business. He was noted for his pioneering work in the development of new printing techniques. His son, Peter Jarrold, one of three brothers who were to manage the business, set up the John Jarrold Printing Museum as a memorial to him.

The ability to adapt to changing circumstances has been a characteristic of Jarrold's right from JJ's move into farming, shipping and printing in the nineteenth century to the decision to move out of the previous core businesses of printing and publishing in the twenty-first. Yet again with moves into property and training the company has shown a capacity for embracing change and taking advantage of opportunities in the wider market. Whatever JJ may have thought of his sons, one can be confident that he would proudly approve the record of succeeding generations in developing the business into which he put so much effort. Today three members of the seventh generation of Jarrolds since the business was founded remain actively involved in the management of the company. Jarrold's remains, and looks set to remain, an integral part of Norwich's commercial scene. Of all the companies reviewed in this book, Jarrold's is probably that which has remained closest to the ideals of its entrepreneurial forefather.

Sources:
Archived material at the Norfolk County Record Office
A Descriptive Account of Norwich 1890
The House of Jarrolds 1823-1923

His sole asset in life to begin with was character.

*A. B. Cooper, in The Sunday at Home
Magazine, May 1909*

John Godfery Howlett (JGH) had had a long week. Leaving
Norwich, as usual, at 6.00 am on Monday morning he had
travelled by horse and trap, calling on customers of the
leather currying business in which his father had invested
heavily, and which he had recently joined. On Saturday, he
had arrived at Bourne in Lincolnshire where he visited an old
customer of the company, Thomas White, the owner of a
shoemaking business of modest size, having about a dozen
employees. White's fourteen-year-old son, George, helped
Howlett bring in his samples of leather, and stayed, listening
intelligently, while his father concluded his negotiations with
Howlett. When the business had been transacted, Thomas
White asked Howlett whether his company, Howlett &
Tillyard, had an opening for which George might be suitable,
as he felt that his own business was not of sufficient size to
merit his joining it, another son already having done so.
George later wondered whether it had actually been his
father's plan that he should train in Norwich but then return
to run the family business.

Howlett promised to take the matter up with his father and the other partners when he returned to Norwich. When he did so, giving a favourable assessment based on his own experience of the boy, it was agreed that George should be offered the role of a junior clerk, which he took up two years later in 1856 on a wage of 8 shillings a week.

This appointment was the start of a quite remarkable career that was to have a profound, and beneficial, effect on the company, on the life of Norwich and arguably on the country as a whole.

The young George White was not just intelligent, he was well informed and, perhaps, a trifle precocious. At the age of twelve it was recorded that he could name the constituency of every MP and he read avidly about politics, having nailed his colours to the Liberal mast.

Although George had been at Bourne Grammar School, Norwich offered wider horizons than Bourne educationally, and George took full advantage of these. Despite his working day at the factory starting at 8 o'clock he was able to squeeze in some study before it. A local solicitor, Mr Dowson, offered, as an act of philanthropy, free tuition in core subjects such as mathematics and languages to youngsters willing to attend before going to work. George attended these for two hours each morning. He also benefited from the proximity to the factory of St Mary's Baptist Church, where the minister, the Revd Gould took an interest in the boy and taught him the art of speaking in public. Gould is said to have been so impressed with his pupil that, even at this early age, he predicted that the young man would enter Parliament.

George remained a clerk for about four years, and was then appointed, as JGH had been before him, a representative. He had shown his ambition when he applied for such a role only a few months previously, only to be turned down on the grounds that he was 'too young'. It appeared to be the policy of the company to ensure that future senior managers had a clear understanding of the market in which the company operated, and a personal connection with its major customers. On his return to a full time role in Norwich, at the age of twenty-five, he was entrusted with the management of the shoe department, possibly as the result of the ill health of one of the partners.

The shoe industry was undergoing great change at the time, and Norwich was in the forefront of its development. In earlier times most places, even small villages, had their own shoemaker. In rural areas the trade was very seasonal as it was only as a result of higher earnings at harvest time that agricultural labourers could afford to kit out their families. Boots and shoes fell into two categories, either 'straights' designed to 'fit' either foot or 'pairs' expensively made to measure.

But times were changing. Retail shoe shops became more evident, and even the first chains of such shops began to appear. They catered for customers who were not content with 'straights' but could not afford custom-built shoes, and thus the production of shoes in a range of pre-determined sizes became common practice.

Norwich, with its traditional textile trade in near terminal decline had a corps of workers who were used to tasks demanding manual dexterity. One of the first manufacturers to cater for this new market was James Smith, who had set up in Norwich, as early as the 1790s, the company which later became Startrite. At the time the manufacture of shoes was undertaken very much in the way that textile work had been traditionally, by people working from home under the orchestration of garret masters. Men cut out the uppers and soles and the stitching was done by women. The garret master then matched soles and uppers, sending them back to the men for shaping and then on to the women for trimming. The whole process was convoluted and wasteful.

Howlett and Tillyard had also seen an opportunity to expand their interests from the provision of leather for bootmakers into manufacturing footwear themselves. In 1846 JGH's father had invested the enormous sum of £10,000 in the leather-curing business of Mr Tillyard. JGH's grandfather had been a wine and spirit merchant in King's Lynn in a relatively small way of business – his estate at the time of his death was valued at about £2,000. It is not clear from where but JGH's father appears to have acquired rather greater wealth. He seems to have been a tenant farmer, in Great Bircham, of about 500 acres at the time of his investment, though he later lived in Sedgeford Hall. As to whether his investment was a result of a long-sighted analysis of the business opportunity or a means of securing employment for his son one cannot be sure. What is clear though is that it enabled a significant expansion in the business and may have funded the later removal to new premises on St George's Plain, where the company was to remain almost to the end.

In a fascinating celebration of the business at the time of its centenary in 1946, F. W. Wheldon regretted how little data remained from the formative period, and was unable to identify precisely the time at which the major emphasis moved from the supply of leather to the manufacture of shoes. Clearly the latter was a significant portion of the business by the time of George White's appointment to manage the process.

By then, although the extremely time-consuming out-working practices continued to be the norm, mechanisation had begun to play a part. Charles Winter, grandson of the James Smith who had set up half a century earlier, was imbued with as much pioneering spirit as his grandfather, bringing in sewing machines capable of 3,000 stitches a minute as early as 1856 and employing steam-driven machinery to stitch soles by 1860. The balance between these policies may initially have been a fine one financially, the obvious benefits of centralised mechanised production being offset to some extent by the savings achieved under the old system as all the outworkers were self-employed, thus neither generating recurring costs at quiet periods, nor requiring the substantial capital outlay needed to install plant. Nor did they result in the capital cost implicit in carrying high levels of stock. Gradually, however, the benefits of centralised production became too significant to ignore. White's own view was, as so often, both economic and moralistic. At the time he started working in the industry he said 'a boot was begun and finished by about three people and the work was all put out and done at home by hand'. By 1909 he explained that the manufacture involved as many as forty hands and was carried out mechanically in the factory. He saw this 'extreme sub-division of labour' as detracting from pride in individual skill but felt positive that the change had brought about improvement in both the moral and physical well-being of the workers.

George White was instrumental in bringing his firm into the modern era, so much so that ten years after his appointment as manager of the shoe department he was invited to become a full partner in the business without being required to invest any capital. Such had been the impression he created from the start that, fifty years after he joined the firm, JGH was to say of him 'he had not been in the business for two years before we were convinced that the young man would become a leader of men, a great help to the firm, and a power in the municipality'. His progress through the firm and the change in the main emphasis of the firm itself is evident from the various census returns. In 1861 he is described as leather merchant's clerk, in 1871 as a manager in a wholesale shoe warehouse. By 1881 he is listed as a wholesale manufacturer and leather merchant and by 1891 as a shoe manufacturer. In the same period his success enabled him to move from a modest terrace home to Bourne Villa on Unthank Road and then to The Grange further along the same road where, by 1891, a domestic staff of three live-in servants looked after him and the six of his daughters who were still living at home.

White formed an effective partnership with JGH who shared with him a strong Baptist faith and a close friendship, no doubt reinforced by the fact that they had married two sisters. White had married Anne Ransome in 1862 and they had a total of eight children, of whom only one was a son and followed him into the business.

In the company there was little doubt who was the dominant partner, White ran the factory while JGH, particularly after the retirement of his father, concerned himself mainly with the financial aspects of the business, White was the driving force, which Howlett acknowledged and seemed content that it should be so.

Howlett and White's shoe factory opposite St George's Church

Both partners were influenced by their Christian beliefs. They often attended chapel on their way to work, and also held prayer meetings at the factory. In today's secular age that may seem strange, but it was really only an extension of the practice in many homes where domestic servants joined in a formal session of family prayers. Certainly both Howlett

and White adopted a paternalistic approach to their employees, so it was natural enough that they should pray
together as well as work together. Life in the factory was
subject to a 'fair but tough' form of discipline. Good time-
keeping was essential and not always easy before the days
when watches were the norm. In fact the firm paid the verger
of nearby St George's to ensure that the church clock was
kept wound up to provide employees with a time check.
Workers were given discs, stamped with their works number,
which they were expected, on arriving at the factory, to throw
into a box which was under the eagle eye of a timekeeper
who, reputedly, was often hit by discs thrown deliberately in a
'careless' manner. Being late by just a minute would result in
the deduction of fifteen minutes pay. Light in the works was
provided first by oil, and later by gas and then electricity; the
machinery was powered by steam and then by electricity. The
partners took their lunch at their desks, brought for them
from home; whether it was still hot after journeys from
Bracondale and Unthank Road respectively must be open to
question. Office staff aped the partners' practice and lunched
at their desks also.

George White's overview was comprehensive – he was not
a delegator in the mould of Colman. Any revision in the
wages of even the most junior employee was entirely at his
discretion and he carried his paternalistic principles so far as
to lead him to advise a representative, whose success had
been rewarded with an unusually large commission payment,
that he ought to leave the money deposited with the company
to earn interest, rather than running the risk of frittering it
away. The company's historian, writing in the 1940s,
recorded that 'the hand and mind of George White
increasingly dominated every section – even the smallest
section – of the business in a remarkable way from the time
he was made a partner'. It is perhaps not surprising that he
also recorded that while JGH was remembered with affection,

George White was recalled rather with respect and admiration.

White had quickly recognised the advantages of centralised production. Cutting out the delays inherent in completing the manufacture by using a number of different outworkers, in a host of locations, significantly improved productivity even without mechanisation. With the use of plant to carry out some tasks, production grew even quicker so that, instead of manufacturing to meet immediate demand, large stocks of finished shoes became available. In fact when the partners' original agreement expired 'through the effluxion of time' to use the words in the replacement deed of 1885, the amount of capital tied up in the stock of shoes and leather, over £23,000 – in excess of £2 million in 2012 values - was more than twice that of the property and the plant.

To a man of White's character there was a special appeal in the centralisation of production, namely the effect on the daily lives of employees. Having himself signed the pledge as far back as 1857 and being an evangelical campaigner for the temperance movement, he was very concerned at the use of alcohol by outworkers. Unused to the disciplined routine of the factory, the outworker's life was wholly dependent on the amount of work the garret master had in hand. Frequent intervals between periods of labour led to what would have been, to White, an undesirable local institution known as 'Cobbler's Monday'[1]. In effect the outworkers, having received their pay for the previous week passed that day spending it in the pubs. Even in Norwich, whose population was less in thrall to the combination of barley and the hop than was the case in many cities, it was still a major problem. For White and his partner the solution lay in regular work within the disciplined environment of a factory, so that their modernisation plans served to increase both profitability and sobriety. A study published in 1910 recorded an improvement in social habits as a result.

Howlett and White, each of whom had, as part of their early experience, worked on the shop-floor, were genuinely concerned with the welfare of their employees, and were not unsympathetic to the organisation of labour. They worked to establish stable wages and a fixed working week. Even this did not protect them in 1897 when 1,500 workers in the industry locally staged a six month strike in support of an unsuccessful demand for a minimum wage. One circumstance of this dispute throws a significant light on the character of George White.

One week the Operatives Union did not manage to deliver the strike pay on which their members depended to provide for their families. The local Union official, James Mason, a fellow Liberal Councillor, approached George White, who personally guaranteed the amount necessary to fill the gap. This was an extraordinary gesture from an employer, and a good employer by contemporary standards. White's generosity of spirit didn't stop there. When the strike was over Mason found himself blacklisted by employers in the industry. White gave him a job and later Mason's son also joined the firm.

The factory interior

81

The company continued to expand rapidly. By the end of the 1880s the partnership had extended to include the sons of both JGH and George White. Both sons were expected to follow the same pattern as their fathers, with immersion in all aspects of the business so as to equip them for management later. The sons were apparently reprimanded by George White on one occasion some years later when, coming into the office at 8.00 a.m. on a Saturday after a late sitting in the Commons the evening before, he found that neither of the younger generation had arrived. Having waited less than patiently for their arrival he greeted their eventual appearance with the words: 'The *workers* in this factory clock in at 8.00 a.m.' before upbraiding them for purchasing new machinery without his prior approva.

Relationships between the generations seem to have remained good however. The partnership had switched to a limited liability company in 1899 and the directors were listed as the two Howletts, father and son, living as neighbours in Bracondale, and the two Whites, father and son, living as neighbours in Unthank Road.

The Premier Export House in Norwich

An Example of a Court Shoe made by Howlett & White, Norwich.

Shoes which give Satisfaction

HOWLETT & WHITE'S shoes give satisfaction because they are made only of the finest materials in a factory which has for over half a century studied and supplied the requirements of Overseas Trade. They are the premier firm in Norwich manufacturing for the High Class Export Trade, and it is largely due to them that Norwich-made goods hold the high reputation they do in the world's markets. Your enquiries are invited.

Howlett & White, Ltd.

St. George's Plain,
NORWICH.

The time was approaching when JGH would retire from the business, but George White continued as Chairman and Managing Director, despite his other onerous responsibilities. By 1910 Howlett & White had become major manufacturers, their shoes selling not just at home, but also exported to South America and all corners of the Empire, employing over 1,200 staff and occupying the largest single building shoe factory in England, manufacturing 200,000 pairs of shoes and boots a year. They made shoes to satisfy a very wide market. The range included fashion shoes for women, practical footwear for men, and children's shoes too. Using innovative machinery to insert spikes in running shoes and to produce a crinkled sole for better grip on the tennis court they became a significant force in all forms of footwear

Quite apart from his business acumen and management skills what distinguished White from the many other non-conformist entrepreneurs of his time was the intensity of his religious beliefs and the avenues up which this intensity led him.

Reference has already been made to his teetotalism. His advocacy of temperance was in part derived from his recognition of the impact on the economic welfare of the country. He attributed a loss of 15 per cent of the working time of individual workers to drink. Not only that, he drew attention to the relativity of wages and profits between his industry and brewing. His own wage bill, he claimed was a multiple of five times his net profit, while that of a particular brewer was the reverse, net profit being four times the wage bill. In 1909 he was on record as saying that 'Nothing has such a serious influence [as drink] on the trade of the country, and I believe that the resuscitation of activity in all kinds of useful manufactures and the securing of a fair wage for the great mass of our artisans would be accomplished more easily and effectually by a reduction in our expenditure for drink than by any other means'. He was known to quote Gladstone's remark that 'the evils of drink were greater than those of war, pestilence and famine combined'. One wonders what he made of Gladstone's introduction, in 1861, just four years after White had signed the pledge, of legislation that allowed restaurants to sell wine without any longer having to obtain a licence from the magistrates.

He certainly practised what he preached. In the Norfolk Record Office in Norwich, there is a leather bound presentation volume with a beautifully illuminated tribute to him, celebrating the 50th anniversary of his having signed the pledge. By that time he was President of the Baptist Total

Abstinence Association who, in making the presentation said they 'rejoiced' with him in 'celebrating the Jubilee'. He was the moving spirit behind a campaign to secure a million new pledges and, although the crusade fell short of its target it did attract several hundred thousand.

He campaigned ceaselessly for his cause, advocating the establishment of reading rooms and similar facilities with only non-alcoholic refreshments. Himself a member of the Reform Club he perhaps realised that the pub might be to the working man what the club was to him, a place for relaxation in congenial company. He certainly knew what the pubs provided. He apparently made a habit of researching them in cities he visited, so that he could campaign against them authoritatively. In an interview with the magazine *Sunday at Home* in 1909 he disclosed that, when he was working as a commercial traveller, others in the same occupation staying in an hotel were in the habit of ordering whatever they wanted to drink, having the cost added to the bill for dinner, and splitting it equally between them. The social niceties within a group of 'commercials' needed to be maintained and his abstinence (and refusal to pay a share of the drinks bill) attracted criticism and actually, on occasion, led to him being excluded from the 'commercial' table. He overcame this exclusion by paying, instead, a surcharge of one shilling for his dinner, thus making a contribution to the total cost without compromising the letter, although perhaps the spirit, of his principles.

His prejudice against alcohol was not just the result of what he saw as the economic consequences of its misuse, though that was a major factor; he estimated that the amount of money spent on alcohol was greater than the total sum of taxation. He was as concerned with the human consequences. He believed that it was the major cause of divorce and the prime reason for the absence of people from church. For him alcohol, and a lack of education, militated against any improvement in the lot of the lower classes. His vision was of a society purged of poverty and social distress.

He was an early proponent of a minimum wage, but tempered his view by reference to the need to ensure that employers paid only what they could without endangering their business. His philosophy is neatly encapsulated in the address he gave on being chosen, in 1904, as President of the Baptist Union:

> 'The wages of any given industry are controlled by laws that appear to be practically inexorable and to exceed these wages say by 5 per cent or 10 per cent would mean failure to the employer, and still greater poverty to the employee, but there is no reason why, other changes working in conjunction, a proper subsistence level for the whole people should not be reached'

That may seem a moderate approach by the standards of the 1970s and 1980s, but at the time these views would have been seen as quite radical. His radicalism extended to a determination to eliminate the privileges of class, the power and influence of the established church, and the grinding poverty experienced by the workers. He was generally pragmatic, though he despised plutocrats and employers such as the brewer referred to above, who paid so poorly while gaining so much. But he favoured a staged approach to redistribution of wealth using benefits such as pensions and state insurance rather than anything more dramatic. Maintaining industry in a sound state was key to maintaining employment, and employment was one key to the welfare of the working class.

An unyielding opponent of privilege, it was his conviction that a further key to eradicating social ills was education, and much of his life was spent in its promotion. Another conviction was that it was the duty of all Christian men to take a part in politics, although he said that if he found that his political duties would prevent him carrying out his religious ones, it would be the politics he would ditch.

He used his political influence, locally to start with, and then nationally, to promote his beliefs about both temperance and education. By the time he was eighteen George White was already secretary of a Liberal Ward Association in Norwich, and he was elected to the Council in 1876. Civic recognition, as Sheriff and Alderman, were to follow, and he led the Norwich Liberal Party for 14 years. He didn't step onto the national stage however until 1900, when he was elected MP for North West Norfolk. His wife had died two years previously, and it may have been that he only then felt more willing to engage at a level that would take him from home even more. Already he travelled extensively to speaking engagements in the cause of Temperance, invariably smartly dressed and sporting a silk hat.

In Norwich he became involved in education quite early and by 1874 he was a member of the Norwich School Board, for fifteen years as its Chairman. The *Eastern Daily Press* wrote, on his death, that he had made 'the education of the children of the working classes possible, and even popular'.

His involvement with education extended to all ages, and to all types of institutions. He had begun to attend Sunday School in Bourne at the age of four and his interest in such schools lasted throughout his life. Towards the end he re-called that within two weeks of arriving at Norwich he had taken a Mission Sunday School meeting in a rough working class neighbourhood. He was sixteen at the time, and his connection with that school continued throughout his life. This was the Sayer Street Mission, built by Peto under the auspices of the City Mission whose supporters included Jarrold and Caley. He recalled a time when 'myself and wife, eight children and three servants locked up house and turned out every Sunday afternoon to attend the Sunday School'.

At St Mary's he was Superintendent of the afternoon Junior School and in 1887, in what he described later as 'one of the best works of my life', he founded the St Mary's Men's First Day Adult School. The curriculum obviously focused on religion and education, but the work went far beyond this, providing a sort of social centre and establishing, as was the case at the factory, a savings bank paying 5 per cent interest and a fund to provide benefits when sick, and coal when needed. It also established, on a self-help basis, a fund to pay an unemployment benefit of five shillings per week, for a subscription of 2d. One benefit that particularly pleased White was the establishment of a 'Goose Club' where sub-scriptions provided a bird for members at Christmas. The establishment of such clubs had been the habit of local publicans and White clearly enjoyed cocking a snook at them, saying that in such cases 'the publican had got the goose while the members got the feathers'. The class had started with thirty-one scholars and by the time he was interviewed in 1909 it had 270. C. B. Jewson in his book on the Baptists of Norfolk provides an engaging picture of the school at work.

> 'In this and other schools gentle ladies from the sheltered homes of the suburbs of Norwich were to be seen bending over the shoulders of rough men from the city's slums, instructing them in the rules of simple arithmetic or the vagaries of English spelling'.

Some of those rough men obviously shared White's radicalism and his forthrightness; when he was elected to Parliament they were reported to be delighted when he was reprimanded by the Speaker.

He was as concerned with vocational training as with basic academic studies, anxious to ensure that education was tailored to enhance the skills of the lower classes to prepare them for employment. As we have seen he believed that settled work with regular pay was a necessary pre-condition of any improvement, and he worked ceaselessly to promote it. On the national stage he continued in the same vein. Elected in 1900, he came to national politics at a time when education was a hot topic, and it was his opposition to the Education Act of 1902 that was to bring him to greater prominence.

His election to Parliament came when he was almost sixty. He could almost certainly have stood earlier; Gladstone had marked him down as a potential candidate for Norwich after hearing him speak some years earlier. White himself expressed reservations about standing in a constituency where he had substantial business interests and thus it was for North West Norfolk, a predominantly agricultural seat that he stood, on the retirement of the redoubtable Joseph Arch. That remarkable demagogue, who had started life as an agricultural worker and Primitive Methodist preacher, was the instigator of the National Agricultural Labourers Union that successfully campaigned for improved pay. On the way he gained the friendship of an improbable but committed supporter, Daisy, Countess of Warwick and long term mistress of Edward VII, who is reputed to have brought Edward, as Prince of Wales, to take tea with Arch in his Warwickshire cottage[2]. Elected to Parliament in 1885, Arch became enough of a public figure to be the subject of a Spy caricature in *Vanity Fair*, although his contributions within Westminster did not appeal to all his union members, some of whom felt that he didn't serve them best by going to Westminster. A rhyme at the time ran:

> Joseph Arch he stole a march,
> Upon a spotted cow.
> He scampered off to Parliament,
> But where is Joseph now?

White, although not greatly knowledgeable on agricultural matters was an admirer of Arch, and was able to convince his supporters that he would represent them effectively, having started his working life as a wage-earner and having long been a believer in trade unionism and a supporter of its growth.

Arrived in Parliament, both his ability to speak effectively and his preoccupation with education were soon noted. It was a time of great debate on the subject, culminating in the Education Act of 1902, introduced by the Conservatives. The purpose of this Act was to reorganise the education system. Two impacts of the detailed plans stuck in White's craw. First the Act presaged the end of school boards such as that on which he had been so active for many years, and placed the responsibility instead on Local Education Authorities. Second, by making all schools the beneficiaries of funding, it effectually subsidised the continuation of religious teaching along lines provided by the established church, since they were the managers of a huge number of schools. Such subsidy was absolute anathema to Baptists like White, who felt it unfair that nonconformists should pay, through their rates, for a type of religious education with which they disagreed.

In Parliament White proposed a policy of passive resistance, suggesting that those who agreed with him should withhold their rates. This notion had great popular appeal and a committee was established to promote it by a friend of White, John Clifford. The initial remedy against non-payment was the seizure of goods. Where such seizure could not be effected imprisonment was a further option and within four years no fewer than 176 nonconformist supporters had been sent to jail and over 70,000 summonses had been issued to those following White's suggestion. He himself had goods seized for non-payment several times.

The effects of this campaign were to propel White further on to the national stage and to move nonconformists into the Liberal camp, aiding a landslide victory in 1906. Disappointingly for him he was not, as some had anticipated, offered a ministerial role in education, but he remained committed to the cause. Even the new Liberal administration was unable to abolish the Education Act in the face of opposition from the House of Lords. Clifford continued his personal policy of passive resistance and was summonsed for the 57th time for non-payment as late as 1922, the year of his death.

White proved an able debater and sufficiently open-minded to look for compromise. He was popular enough among his nonconformist colleagues to be chosen as their leader, but it was probably on his home turf, in Norwich, where he was a commanding figure in both local industry and politics, that he had most influence.

George White died in 1912, in Norwich, of lung cancer, radium treatment in London having proved ineffective. His last words suggesting almost an impatience to be with his God were 'What are we waiting for?' There can be little doubt that he was genuinely mourned by thousands. Over three thousand were said to have been present for his interment (at the Rosary, like Colman and Jarrold) and these included representatives of all churches, even those which he had vigorously opposed in his lifetime.

Sir George White – he was knighted in 1907 – was, beyond question, a remarkable man. Despite his business success he was, first and last, an evangelical Christian. His espousal of the causes of temperance and education led him into prodigious efforts to facilitate social change, which, combined with a punishing six days a week work schedule, even before he entered Parliament, left him little time for leisure. He took up golf at the age of sixty and claimed to have been a useful cricketer in his youth, but how he found the time to indulge such pursuits is hard to see. A description of his normal Sunday included the Adult School at St Mary's from nine o'clock, followed by the public service involving him both as a deacon and a seat steward until noon. By two o'clock it was time for his Sunday School, followed by a Prayer Meeting, and then Evening Service.

In the field of education he achieved much locally; at peak his school board was responsible for the education of over 15,000 local children and he worked hard to ensure that they not only became literate but also developed wider horizons than they would have done without schooling. When made a Freeman of Norwich in 1910 it marked his 'earnest and untiring labour for the upraising of the people, particularly in the advancement of education'. He was also an early supporter of 'day release' to enable his employees to improve their prospects, and was heavily involved, as was Colman, with the formation and development of the Norwich YMCA. It is certainly fitting that, more than a hundred years after his death his contribution to local education is still recognised by the existence of a school in Norwich, bearing his name.

As a businessman and manager he was extraordinarily successful, earning the plaudits of his partners and the respect of his employees. He was probably the most significant of Norwich's many shoe manufacturers and certainly a leader in modernising the industry. Unlike some contemporaries, he clearly cared about the welfare of his employees and sought to improve their lives, and he recognised the downside of the separation of labour and the effect of the loss of individual skills which that implied. He sought to improve their lives by the provision of secure employment, regular and adequate wages, and some degree of protection in hard times. A very paternalistic employer, he also established such extramural attractions as sports clubs and a company band, even if he was some way behind Colman in the matter of providing facilities for the workers to have lunch. As late as 1909 he was expressing the hope that the company could make such provision at some time in the future. Paternalism may sometimes be viewed as a technique employed by managers to maintain a compliant workforce, but in this case it seems to have been driven by a genuine desire to improve the lot of the men. For White, such improvement meant not just regular employment at a fair wage, but also an improvement in their mode of living, brought about by temperance and healthy attitudes, leading to an increased closeness to the church. He may have been Christian and paternalistic, but he was no pushover. In 1896 his employees sought a general wage increase. His response betrayed some irritation:

'The workmen have very properly demanded that workshops should be provided to save their cottages from the noise and dirt of trade; we respond and build with every convenience for their comfort, and the men turn round and say we can afford to pay this large advance, because we can build new warehouses'.

He was strongly in favour of the centralised management of essential services such as water, gas and electricity. He was the enemy of privilege which he saw as the natural result of Conservative politics and Anglicanism, and determined to eliminate it. For all his reforming zeal he was not a hair-shirt radical; he lived in very comfortable circumstances in a large property with the usual trappings, such as a billiard room, and resident domestic staff. Much more a Fabian than a Tribunite, his militancy was tempered with pragmatism. Successful companies meant a buoyant economy, which in turn led to full employment and thus to opportunities for improvement in the lifestyle of their employees. These would lead to a better ordered society, better health, better education, more universal allegiance to the Christian, especially the Baptist, faith.

On a personal level the respect he seems universally to have earned may not always have been coupled with affection, except amongst those who knew him best, such as his scholars at the Adult Day School, his partners and his family. But he was always keen to reward self-improvement and initiative. In 1886, a key employee, Henry Sexton, resigned taking three of his sons who also worked with White with him. He planned to start up in business on his own and he found that the first customer to place an order was none other than George White.

White was not a man with whom it would have been likely to have been easy to have a simply social conversation. His use of humour was sufficiently rarely evident for one example to feature in the Norvic history. It was said that, after half a lifetime on the local hustings it was only when he came to stand for Parliament that he risked, for the first time, a 'platform joke'. He told the story of a married man who sent a telegram to the family doctor, which ran 'Mother in law at the gate of death – come and pull her through'. Humour was not perhaps his strong point. What his fellow representatives, well lubricated with the alcohol for which he had helped indirectly to pay, made of his conversation at those dinners at the 'Commercial's table' in the hotels may be imagined.

Perhaps his own assessment of his philosophy is implicit in his reply when made a Freeman. 'The best test as to whether we have rightly used our experience of life is to be found in the width and force of our sympathies for the lives and struggles of others, and in our consequent ability and willingness to help them. I can honestly say that I have prospered in material circumstances; I am conscious that by keeping in touch with the poor and the workers, my interest is as deep as at any time in my life'.

There can have been few men, especially those who have enjoyed such commercial success, who have maintained without hesitation such an earnest and disciplined commitment to their beliefs, or worked so untiringly to promote them. While he may not have been the ideal dinner companion, he was certainly a figure who commands deep respect and admiration. As *The Times* recorded in his obituary on May 13th 1912:

> 'Sir George White was a plain and modest man, who found greatness thrust upon him. He made no pretensions to brilliance, but he was an adept at business, and his character deserved the respect which his fortune would in any case have received.'

Postscript

As we have seen, the sons of both partners followed their fathers into the business, and Howlett's younger son joined later. They continued to run it on lines of which their fathers would surely have approved. Not only was a pension scheme for the employees introduced as early as 1920, but Sir George's son, followed his father's example in local affairs, serving both as Sheriff and, later as Lord Mayor of Norwich, as well as being a JP. Politically he became the leader of the local Liberal Party in 1920. He too was honoured with a knighthood, in 1932.

The business continued to expand, absorbing a number of smaller firms. The Norvic brand was introduced to facilitate a national advertising campaign in about 1913 and by 1935 all the diverse brands of the other companies within the group were brought under its umbrella. At that time something in the order of 15 per cent of the whole workforce of Norwich were engaged in the boot and shoe industry, and Norvic began to take its own distribution in house by purchasing retail outlets.

The company was still thriving at its centenary in 1946 and on into the 1960s. Under imaginative management it was an early user of television advertising and sought to capture different markets, for example by employing 1956 Olympic Swimming Gold Medallist, Judy Grinham, to tap the teenage market.

However, profits began to fall towards the end of the 1960s and early 1970s and in 1971 Norvic was taken over by an investment company. This was the high noon of the asset-stripper and all 140 Norvic shops were promptly sold off to Timpsons. A condition of the deal was that Timpsons would continue to sell only Norvic products for the next three years. At the end of that time the deal was not renewed and Norvic lost overnight something in the order of a quarter of its UK sales. It struggled on for a few more years before going into administration in 1981, a sad end for a pioneering and old established business.

[1] This seems to have been quite a wide practice. St Crispin was the patron saint of shoemakers, and Thomas Wright, in his book *The Romance of the Shoe*, published in 1922, recounts the following anecdote: 'This is not St Crispin's day' remonstrated somebody, one Monday, to a shoemaker who was sitting in his cups. 'Sir' came the reply, 'the anniversary of St Crispin is the first Monday in every week'.

[2] Although Joseph Arch was not elected to Parliament until 1885, he had been active in Norfolk for many years before that. The following is an extract from the diary of my great grandfather, the High Church Vicar of East Dereham, on April 6th 1875.
'After Evensong dropped into the Corn Hall to hear the famous Mr. Arch who was haranguing a vast concourse of labouring men to join the Union. Arch was a farmer's labourer and is now a paid delegate for the union all over England. He is a thickset coarse sort of man of about 40. His address was decidedly revolutionary. He let off the Church better than I expected. A few of our small democratical people were on the platform, dissenting shopkeepers, and frequently cried 'That's it!' when any telling remark was made by the speaker. The heat was intolerable and I felt green all evening from the steam arising from so many with whom cleanliness is not always accounted next to godliness.'

Sources:
A Norvic Century, F. W. Wheldon, Jarrold & Sons, Norwich & London, 1946
'Business, Tact & Thoroughness – A History of the Norvic Shoe Company' David Jones, *Journal of the Norfolk Archaeological Society*, 1986
The Story of the Norwich Boot and Shoe Trade, Frances & Michael Holmes, Norwich Heritage Projects 2013
'Through the Windows of a Baptist Meeting House', Barry M. Doyle, in the *Baptist Quarterly* 1996
'Education and the Liberal Rank and File in Edwardian England: The Case of Sir George White', Barry M. Doyle in the *Liberal Democrat History Group Newsletter*, September 1996

'Sir George White of Norwich', A. B. Cooper in *The Sunday at Home Magazine* May 1909

The Times Digital Archive

The Eastern Daily Press Archive in the Millennium Library, Norwich.

The Baptists in Norfolk, C. B. Jewson, Carey Kingsgate Press, 1957

The Spectator Archive

Under the Parson's Nose, C. S. Armstrong (ed) The Larks Press 2012

Two pages from *The Rising Son* (see p.8) showing the favoured son ready to begin his career as a banker, and a complaisant Board welcoming a generous dividend.

Sir Robert Harvey's Mausoleum in Kirby Bedon churchyard

i

Thomas Bignold

THEATRE OF HUMBUG,

NEAR THE

LIFE OFFICE PUMP,

SURRY STREET.

The Public are respectfully informed, that on Thursday next, the 30th July 1835, there will be performed at the above place, at 12 o'clock at noon, the Farce of

Blindman's Buff;

OR,

HOCUS POCUS,

under the direction of that experienced Manager

Master Sammy,

who will not only go through various manœuvres himself, but will shew how he has performed the part of *various defunct persons*, during the last 15 years !!!

SCENE 1st. Will exhibit the extraordinary progress of

SAMMY'S FATHER,

from the time he gave his son the Pistols to defend the Books and Parchments, to the happy period of his high career as a

Master Shoe-maker

in Blackfriars road, London. Whilst in this business it will be seen how nearly his beloved son escaped Strangling, and he himself a serious prosecution, as it was only through the happy construction of the

Life Office Pump

that both were miraculously saved. It is said however that the Pump sustained damage to the amount of £40,000, by the imprudent management on this occasion.

After the first Scene will be introduced Sammy's famous performance of the

THIMBLE RIG,

by which it will be shewn that Parchments, Deeds, Mortgages, &c., either *are, or are not* the Conjurors.
It is said that this Rig has answered exceedingly well, in preventing *improper curiosity* on the part of vulgar creditors at BANKruptcy meetings, &c.

After this naturally comes the after piece of

RAISING the WIND,

shewing how easy it is to make a JOINT STOCK PIE *appear* SOUND and WHOLE, when it is in fact ALL TO SHATTERS !! This is effected by an unseen Current *constantly setting in* from the *Life Office Pump !!!*
IN SCENE 2nd. A most extraordinary trick recently **discovered** by SAMMY, will be exhibited.—Aaron's Rod swallowing up all the Rods of the Egyptians was a wonder—but Sammy will make

Twelve Buckram Men out of Three,

each with perfect head, arms, body, and legs. The public will really take them for twelve real men—but they are so at the mercy of the Arch conjuror, that he can with one Stroke of his magic wand, reduce them to the original three again : who as before will live, move and have their being at the command of Sammy.

As this last performance is not merely of local interest, a full account of it will be published for the benefit of Insured persons from the Land's End to John o'Groat's House : as it is a trick quite unparalleled in the Hocus Pocus Art.

CAUTION.

Although the Theatre has been fresh decorated for the occasion, and the *Manager* has done his best to PROP and BOLSTER it up for fear of accidents ;—it is however not SAFE for the *admission of the Public.* The *patronage* prop, of ASH-ley, has lately been withdrawn.

This is certain that the performance of

A PAS DE TROIS

by a NOWHERE, a STARLING, and a CROW, will be the last time of their appearing on the boards.

N. B. *Tickets may be had at the Silky Booth.*

A spoof playbill to lampoon the Norwich Union

A partial view of The Grange, Unthank Road, home of
Sir George White

iv

Advertisement by Alfred Munnings

Alfred Munnings' painting of the Caley stalls at the Leipzig Fair

Lid of a box of Caley's chocolates

Colman's Mustard and Starch advertisements

Colman's railway van, now at the Museum at the Holt terminus of the North Norfolk Railway

John Patteson in his militia uniform

Jeremiah James Colman (1830-1898)
Mustard Manufacturer, Member of Parliament, Social Reformer

The unwritten yet ever intelligible and interesting annals of the industry and commerce of Great Britain, rich as they are in evidence of the energy, ability and enterprise which have been principal factors in establishing the nation's mercantile greatness, present to our notice few such instances of uninterrupted progress and expansion as that incorporated in the history of J & J Colman.

A Descriptive Account of Norwich, published by Robinson, Son and Pike, Brighton. c.1890

Twenty years after Colman's began to manufacture mustard at Stoke Mill near Norwich in 1814, just one man, Lazarus Horne, was needed to pack the entire output into casks for distribution to the retail outlets. He was able to do so despite having only one arm, the other having been lost in an accident at the mill. By 1880, nearly 12,000 railway wagons were needed to deal with the 927,229 casks and boxes of mustard despatched from the works at Carrow.

This huge growth was attributable largely to one man, Jeremiah James Colman, a quite remarkable visionary patriarch, whose 44 years managing Colman's turned a small business into a vast organisation with worldwide distribution and a string of Royal Warrants from Queen Victoria, the Prince of Wales, the King of Italy and the Emperor of France.

The company had been founded by his great uncle Jeremiah, who, having no children of his own, adopted his nephew, Jeremiah James's father. Jeremiah senior had begun business as a miller in 1804 but, ten years later moved to Stoke Holy Cross, where he purchased an existing mill which had been used for the production of paper and mustard, and in May 1814 he advertised in the *Norfolk Chronicle* that:

> having taken the Stock and Trade lately carried on by Mr EDWARD AMES, (he) respectfully informs his Customers and the Public in general that he will continue the Manufacturing of Mustard.

It seems therefore that the move into mustard was more opportunistic than strategic, and the scale remained small. By 1823 Jeremiah had brought James into the business, which became 'J & J Colman'. In the 1830s total employees numbered about thirty; James himself mixed and sifted the mustard flour while his wife and daughter labelled the casks filled by the one-armed Mr Horne.

Not much more than a cottage industry at this stage Colman's grew fast and by the time that Jeremiah James had taken control of manufacturing in the mid-1850s the number of staff had grown to 200. He had joined the company, aged seventeen, and in 1851 was appointed a partner at the age of twenty-one. His father died in 1854, leaving Jeremiah James (JJ) in sole charge of the Norwich end of the business. He had inherited from his parents both a devotion to the Baptist faith and a strong sense of his responsibilities as an employer.

By the 1880s the firm had grown so large it had more than 2,000 employees in Norwich, and it was believed that the trickle-down effect of the company's activities was responsible

98

for more than 4,000 other jobs in the city. JJ was not just an exceptionally astute businessman, but also an exceptionally caring employer. In today's post-paternalist employment market the breadth of the services he provided for his staff seems incredible, yet he was not untypical of his time. Sandwiched between Titus Salt and William Hesketh Lever, Colman emerges as one of the great philanthropic, enlightened business leaders of nineteenth century Britain, along with Cadbury, Rowntree and several others. All shared a strong religious conviction – predominantly characterised by nonconformist or Quaker allegiances and all appear to have possessed what might later have been recognised as a large dose of the protestant work ethic.

From the beginning Colman was conscious of the responsibilities resting on his shoulders. Shortly after taking charge he wrote to his mother acknowledging that his task would not always be 'smooth work' being 'at so young an age, master absolutely and unreservedly over so many people'.

A prerequisite for the rapid growth of Colman's under JJ was the move to a larger site. Stoke was small and at a distance from Norwich and thus both inconvenient in terms of communication and unlikely to provide an adequate pool of potential employees. In 1850 the partnership purchased land in Norwich, at Carrow; it was an inspired choice of location, with both railway and river transport immediately to hand, and a large population of potential employees close by. A review of 1890 referred to the works having 'a double line of railway (with sidings and turntables) laid in direct communication with the main lines of the Great Eastern Railway system'. The decision to buy this land has been attributed largely to JJ but whether his was the significant voice in the decision seems doubtful – he was not brought into the partnership until the following year. What is clear, however, is that he managed the move itself, because by the time the Carrow Mustard Mill was built, in 1854, he was, following the death of his father, the only Norwich-based partner. The move to Carrow was not finally completed until 1862.

Carrow House

His business acumen was evident in many ways, especially in his flair for marketing. He also possessed the ability to recognise opportunities, integrate them in a coherent strategy, and choose his senior managers shrewdly, enabling him confidently to delegate detail without losing sight of the essentials.

His appreciation of the value of brand awareness was clear from the start. Indeed, when one considers how the many millions expended in the twenty-first century are used to promote and reinforce brands, the most obvious difference from Colman's activities in the nineteenth is not the message itself, nor even the techniques used, it is simply the range of vehicles available for delivering it. Exactly what Colman would have made successively of television advertising, of the internet and of so-called 'social media' it is impossible to say, but one can be confident that he would have embraced them early, used them effectively and profited greatly.

By 1850 he was already experimenting with the packaging of the product: tins and pots of a size suitable for individual customers and clearly branded 'Colman's' began to replace the anonymous casks. Corporate colours were eye-catching red printed on a yellow field – none of the subtle tones loved by marketing experts today. According to an internal memo written by Colman many years later (1871) the trademark Bull's Head was 'no doubt first used in 1855'. It is still in use today - not many trademarks last 59 years, let alone 159. The earlier casks had just contained a small label which the grocer could use if he chose, which read 'When ordering mustard, make sure you get Colman's'.

Colman was quick to capitalise on any opportunity to promote the product; each award of a Royal Warrant was rapidly incorporated in the label, as were prizes won at international exhibitions. He was keen to ensure that exposure in such exhibitions didn't put at risk Colman's manufacturing secrets. For the Great Exhibition in 1851, he despatched a foreman to the exhibition to maintain the Colman machinery on show. The foreman was instructed not to give away anything about the company to visitors. So faithfully did he comply that one visitor complained to JJ that the company's representative at the Exhibition 'appeared to know nothing about the manufacture of mustard'. That was a little unfair; nobody had told the foreman that the visitor in question was JJ's Uncle Jeremiah!

One of the most effective means of promoting the brand came from leveraging the value of the transport used to despatch goods from Carrow. The Railway & Canal Traffic Act of 1854 permitted companies to use their own rolling stock on the railways. The 12,000 trucks leaving Carrow annually by 1880 all bore the red branding 'Colman's Mustard Traffic' on the yellow field. Trains comprising only trucks bearing the brand were ubiquitous and thus seen not just by customers but by the public at large. A retiring director, writing a retrospective in the works magazine,

Colman's Mustard Train 1895

described these trains, as sometimes comprising more than 170 wagons. Even the wagons of incoming trains bringing fuel for the mill bore the slogan 'Coal for Colman's Mustard Works'.

In the 1870s Colman set up an advertising department, split in two sections, one to handle advertising within the retail outlets and the other to handle 'outdoor advertising'. These were followed by the addition of a printing department to provide product labels (in 1880 for the first time specially decorated labels were introduced for the Christmas trade) and the enamel signs used to promote the range at railway stations and other public sites.

For shopkeepers there were display cards 'Colman's Mustard, the largest manufacturers in the world'. A range of promotional novelties was developed, pencils, matchbox holders, and pipe bowls. One of the most bizarre of these wasn't manufactured until after Colman's death – a 'Zeppelin Raid Detector' which purported, when such factors as wind direction and cloud cover were input, to be able to ascertain the likelihood of a raid.

Colmans were as aware as many companies are today of the value of targeting children. It wasn't until shortly after JJ's death that schools were provided with display cabinets and educational wall-charts on subjects such as British Birds, but for many years before that children had been targeted directly with illustrated booklets of fairy stories, instructions on useful recreations and even early comic strips. Books were issued every Christmas from the 1880s, inscribed 'With Xmas greetings to our young friends all over the world from J & J Colman Ltd'.

Colman's Factory 1890

Colman, along with Lever, was one of the first to recognise the importance of advertising in growing his business, and his establishment of a separate advertising department at a time when the number of administration staff was tiny – in 1864 there were just nine clerks - is clear evidence of this. He was certainly ahead of his time. Not all manufacturers shared his enthusiasm for marketing. Lever, who did, when challenged by a sceptic who doubted the value of branding, asked his challenger what mustard he used. The sceptic replied

'Colman's of course. Is there another?' Lever's point was made, the success of branding was clear, the words mustard and Colmans had come to mean the same thing. A similar phenomenon was evident later, when 'Vacuum Cleaner' and 'Hoover' became synonymous – at least until a later Norfolk-bred entrepreneur, Sir James Dyson, broke that particular mould. Colman's marketing proved so successful that the volume of orders became a problem. In 1872, he recorded that there were 1,392 outstanding invoices 'We were never in such a mess before and I hope never to be again'.

Colman recognised that better control could be exerted, and better profits made, by bringing as much of the process as possible in-house. Apart from the printing department, he also established a plant for manufacturing the tins in which the mustard was sold. If at all possible, nothing went to waste. Colman's didn't just produce mustard; flour, starch and washing blue were also products, and for all of them, the company manufactured on site their own packaging, barrels and tins. The product labels and office stationery were not just printed at Carrow, the paper on which they were printed was manufactured there. Even the coffins for deceased employees were manufactured on site. One trade begat another; perhaps the ultimate example was the use of the waste, grain from the mill and rice from the starch, to feed a herd of pigs, slaughtered at Christmas to provide dinner for the employees and their families.

These pigs give a clue to the growth of the Colman enterprise. In 1856, 140 pigs were slaughtered to provide Christmas dinners; by 1859 the number was 220, said to provide dinner for 2,000 people. As Colman wrote to his wife in December 1856, his employees would 'though they have not a Xmas dinner of turkey and its accompaniments, get something quite as savoury'. At little more than ten helpings per pig, appetites must have been keen!

Colman had married his second cousin, Caroline Cozens-Hardy, of Letheringsett Hall in 1856. She would have been

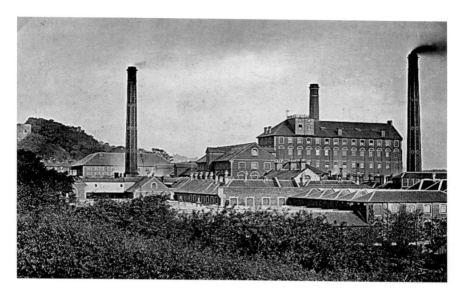

Carrow Works, 1900

under no illusions as to the nature of her husband's commitment to Carrow; during their engagement a letter he wrote to her spelt out his philosophy, 'Influence position and wealth are not given for nothing, and we must try and use them as we would wish at the last we had done...'

Such sentiments were the key to Colman's character. Born into a family with strong non-conformist beliefs to which he adhered throughout his life, he was a deacon of St Mary's Baptist Chapel in Norwich for nearly ten years, although he later became a Congregationalist. He was a serious young man, his interests, outside the chapel and the works, showed no sign of frivolity; he was a member of the Norfolk and Norwich Microscopical Society and an enthusiast about music and natural history. Later he was to give talks to employees on subjects such as 'Sea Anemones' and the 'Habits and Instincts of Animals'.

Having married Caroline at the school in Holt, no local chapel being available, they returned from honeymoon, and moved into Carrow House at the edge of the site. One of their first acts was to host a dinner for 600 employees. Caroline Colman proved the perfect person to give practical application to Colman's paternalist ideas.

Education was of particular interest to them both. Even before the move to Carrow a school had been set up at Stoke Mill with twenty pupils under the tutelage of a Miss Maria Cogman, described as 'a kind old body'. By 1866 the school was at Carrow, initially still under the care of Miss Cogman, and had grown to 200 pupils and to 324 by 1870. It was not until 1880, that compulsory school attendance was introduced from the age of five, so the Colmans were, as in many other respects, ahead of the game. There was a great emphasis on practicality in all that was taught, self-help being central to the Colman philosophy. As well as such subjects as cookery, gardening, bee-keeping, and ironwork, there was Sloyd (derived from the Swedish for handicraft) which was believed to encourage an industrious character and moral behaviour. Strangely the 1861 Census shows Miss Cogman living with the family at Carrow, listed under 'Condition' as a servant but under 'Occupation' as an Infant Schoolteacher.

Although Colman was suspicious of government interference, writing in 1858 to deplore the idea of government 'meddling' in the provision of education, he found an ally in his concentration on manual training in the person of the new Schools Inspector, a Revd Synge[1] who greatly encouraged such developments.

The emphasis on self-help extended to the provision of education, as it did to many of the other benefits Colman introduced for his workers. The opportunity to benefit was provided, but the user had to contribute. A payment had to be made for the provision of schools (1d per week for one child, 1½ d for two and 2d for three from one family). The money was used to fund prizes, Colman having paid all other costs. Other benefits also required the employee to contribute by way of premiums to either the company's insurance scheme or that of a Friendly Society. Colman largely defrayed the cost and employees enjoyed significant benefits, but they had to earn the right by making some provision themselves, albeit at a very favourable rate. This encouragement to make responsible provision for their dependants was consistent with the philosophy of the contemporary 'guru', Samuel Smiles, most simply described in his own words: 'Life will always be, to a large extent, what we make it ourselves'.

The practical provision of welfare was very much in the hands of Caroline Colman. In this she followed in the footsteps of her mother-in-law who had undertaken a similar role in the earlier days of the company. It was one that was consistent with her own attitudes and beliefs. At that time, the proportion of the workforce who were women was much higher in Norwich than was the case nationally. This is probably explained by the nature of manufacturing industry in Norwich. Products such as those of Colman, mustard, starch and washing blue, were by now sold in small units, requiring a large number of staff to carry out the work of packing – a role generally carried out by women. The provision of appropriate facilities to ensure both the physical and moral welfare of these workers was a major objective. A special welfare worker was appointed and appropriate accommodation found for them. Provision was made for them to enjoy breakfast and dinner in a room separate from that provided for the young men; even the playgrounds for boy and girl employees were segregated.

But the Colmans did not restrict their support to their female staff. From the earlier days at Stoke the schools had also been available for classes for the adult workers in the evenings. Meals were provided at cost for all employees and a weekly menu was set out (dumpling and gravy or a pint of scotch broth on Mondays at 1d each and stew, dumpling and vegetables on Fridays for 2d). In the year ended March 1901, the number of dinners provided exceeded 41,000 and over

44,000 pints of coffee and nearly 61,500 pints of tea had been served.

A dispensary was opened in 1864, and a Doctor Fox attended on alternate days. Colman broke entirely new ground when he appointed the country's first female industrial nurse, a Miss Phillippa Flowerday. She had trained at the Norfolk & Norwich Hospital, which moved to a new site outside the city in 2003. The old site was then re-developed for housing, and her memory secured by one of the new streets being named after her. Her role went beyond working with the doctor; she also carried out home visits to sick employees.

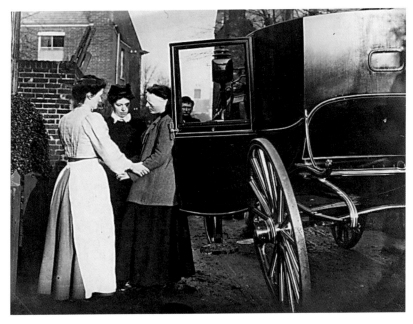

Colman's ambulance

One cannot pretend that employment at Colman's was, by modern standards, comfortable. Working hours in the early days were from 6.00 a.m. to 6.00 p.m. with half an hour for breakfast and an hour for lunch. On Saturdays, work finished an hour earlier, giving a basic working week of sixty-two hours. Overtime was frequently necessary too, and in the early days conditions were not ideal. The lighting was originally provided by burning mustard oil; it was difficult to see across the room for the smoke. Children of eight or nine were employed, but had to spend at least one half day per week at the school the company established.

Even as late as the 1870s, by which time the office staff had grown to 31, it was the habit of the then General Manager, Mr Harvard, to deal firmly with any workers not pulling their weight. As recalled in the Works Magazine 45 years later 'woe betide any individual that sought relaxation in a temporary cessation of work, for, were Mr Harvard in close proximity he was wont to apply the end of a knotted rope to any exposed portion of the body'. However the company did seek to modernise in some ways; it was the proud user of one of the first long distance direct telephone connections between its offices in Norwich and London. How useful it was may be open to question; initially it was said that, while 'it was difficult to distinguish speech, the sustained note of a musical instrument played in the Cannon Street office could be heard distinctly in Norwich'. The test was a cornet solo played by a member of the Works' band.[2] (To those of us accustomed to holding on, listening to Vivaldi, while waiting, often in vain, for a response from a human being, that sounds depressingly familiar.)

It is difficult to get an accurate picture of what it was like to work at Colman's in the 19th century, partly because the world of work has changed so much that what may seem hard to us was not seen in that way then. The difficulty is compounded because most contemporary reports were either sponsored by the firm itself, or simply written in such a respectful, even eulogistic, way as to make them unreliable. In an anonymous booklet, printed in 1901(but probably produced by Colman's own advertising department) the writer describes the site as 'a self-contained town of ceaseless activity'. Fair enough, but then he reports that 'The Carrow Girl is an Institution... there are no white-faced weary toilers at Carrow Works. Every girl takes a lively interest...she is clean and smart and healthy. She dresses simply and neatly, her bare arms and rosy cheeks look none the worse for the tinge of yellow powder that they bear', and continues 'I remarked on their quickness and neatness to one of their good-humoured grey-bearded supervisors'. Moving from the packing department to despatch he marvels at the destinations, Auckland, Los Angeles, Calcutta, and Port Elizabeth, concluding that 'The North American Indian knows the taste and excellence of it' (Colman's mustard). 'The Chinaman finds it an excellent condiment with his bird's nests à la mode'. It seems unwise to place too much reliance on such documents.

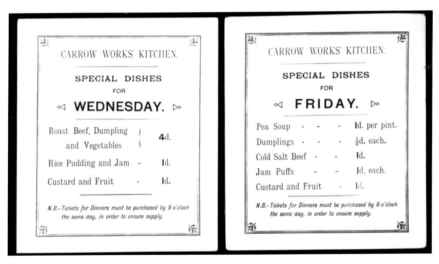

There can be little doubt that JJ himself saw the potential benefit of good public relations. In 1862, he devoted an entire day to showing round the works a representative of *The Grocer* magazine. The resulting 5th April edition was fulsome in its comments on everything, from JJ 'the resident partner receives me with the unstrained courtesy which is so characteristic of an English gentleman' to the premises, which the writer saw as an 'unmistakeable sign of modern activity and enterprise' and which filled him with 'intense satisfaction as incontestable evidence of England's progress'.

What does seem to be beyond doubt is that, by the standards of the day, Colman's was in JJ's time, a model employer. To the modern eye parts of his approach may seem patronising but it is improbable his workers thought so at the time. Paternalism was much more comfortable than the alternatives, and the many benefits he introduced were of a nature which made for a healthier, safer, more secure life. Whether deliberate or not, a result of his policies was to make the individual worker identify with his employer rather than his peers, thus reducing the pressure for labour to organise. Despite this JJ was, unlike many contemporary employers, willing to recognise Trade Unions, but the company reportedly discouraged their representatives tactically, for example by disadvantaging activists by moving them to less well paid posts. There was even an early example of the Japanese practice of later times in the development of company songs to express 'shafu' (company spirit); for the counting house Christmas dinner of 1892, these words were written to be sung to the tune of 'Red, White & Blue', the result being called 'The Good Ship Carrow'.

> Then Hurrah for our trim gallant ship
> We're proud to belong to the crew
> May she sail round the wide world to scatter
> Our mustard, our starch, Flour and Blue

JJ did not limit his beneficence just to Carrow. Some of his generosity benefited a wider audience. Premises he donated were used not just for his employees but for a wider group. He seemed amused that a concert he sponsored in the schoolroom in 1856, which attracted an audience of 300, was attended by no less than four parsons. For a committed and

111

prominent Baptist at a time when feelings between the established church and the nonconformists ran particularly high such a deputation clearly appealed to his sense of humour 'I certainly was surprised to see the white chokers at a concert held at the Stoke Mills Schoolroom, belonging to and lent by a Dissenter.'

He was exceptionally generous to his home city, purchasing, in memory of his wife, the land to extend the children's hospital, bequeathing his collection of paintings to the museum and taking a leading part in the launch of the *Eastern Daily Press*. In 1878 he bought the cricket ground at Lakenham for the use of both Colman's and Norfolk County Cricket Club, who had already played there for over fifty years. Lazarus Horne, the one-armed mustard packer had died in 1851, but his grandson, George Lazarus Horne, played cricket for Norfolk (only once – he didn't trouble the scorers) and must have enjoyed the beautiful ground, which continued to be used by the county until the year 2000. JJ's late father would have been pleased too. Clearly cricket was something of a tradition in the Colman family because, in 1845 he had arranged a number of fixtures between a team comprising only family members and various teams, including the villagers of Letheringsett. JJ's great grandson, Sir Timothy Colman, recounts a family story to the effect that the team did comprise only family members but, in order to get a full XI, had to include a relation who had a wooden leg. He was asked to keep wicket. The Colmans obviously had a strong bowling line-up: Letheringsett, who were boosted by some players from Holt, were dismissed for 16 in the first innings and 27 in the second, the Colman family running out winners by seven wickets. A further fixture was arranged for the following year, hosted by JJ's future father-in-law. This time the game fizzled out in a draw, Letheringsett scoring 77, conceding a first innings lead of 16. The biggest contribution, 20, came from extras, perhaps a consequence of fielding a one-legged wicketkeeper. Jeremiah took seven wickets. Probably no-one was too upset that the game could not be completed for, as the *Norfolk News* reported 'at half past 2 o'clock the company sat down to a sumptuous entertainment, prepared by Mr & Mrs Hardy'.

It wasn't just the big gestures that showed both JJ's generosity and his consideration. In 1882 the missionary the Revd R. F. Guyton returned on leave from India to St Mary's which sponsored him. Before he went back to Delhi Colman presented him with a tricycle, complete with canopy to protect him from the glare, and a 'cage' to carry his books and bedding.

JJ's public life involved two terms as Sheriff and one as Mayor of Norwich. He was appointed a Deputy Lieutenant for Norfolk and an Alderman of Norwich, as well as serving as a magistrate, a trustee of the municipal charities and as Chairman of the governors of Norwich School. He was elected as a Liberal MP in 1871 and represented Norwich for

Photograph taken at the Fête given to celebrate the coming-of-age of JJ's eldest son, Russell J. Colman

24 years. So universal was his popularity that it was said that 'the Tories opposed him in an apologetic manner'. Generally a consistent supporter of Gladstone, with whom he became friendly, he nonetheless helped to scupper Gladstone's ambitions for Irish Home Rule, possibly because of his disapproval of the Irish leader Parnell on the grounds of the latter's adultery. Gladstone stayed more than once with the Colmans at their seaside home at Corton near Lowestoft, the last time in 1891, during which visit the Gladstones learned of the death of their son. Gladstone reciprocated, entertaining JJ at Hawarden as late as 1896 - Gladstone must have forgiven Colman his opposition to Home Rule. They had much in common, not least a taste for theological books, which they used to exchange with each other. Sadly another shared experience was the premature loss of a son. In 1897 Colman, a widower since 1895, travelled with his consumptive son Alan to Egypt for the sake of the latter's health. At Luxor, Alan died. In the following year, 1898, came the death of his mother, and he himself died, at Corton, a few days later.

Drawing of George White, Lord Kimberley, Colman (below) and Gladstone on a visit to Carrow.

Rarely can a captain of industry have been so widely mourned. A tribute to him made at a memorial service described the bringing of his body, by special train, back to Norwich for burial. 'When the mournful cortège left Corton for Somerleyton, the windows of every house were shaded, and everyone was outside to pay the last token of respect to his memory.' On arrival in Norwich, 'all the way from Thorpe station to Princes Street Chapel the road was lined by thousands, and a more orderly and respectful crowd never stood in our streets'. The cortège included 'many wagons laden high with wreaths and tributes' and 'nearly half the 3,000 strong workforce followed on foot while the rest lined the streets'.

Clearly JJ was an extremely shrewd and successful businessman. He achieved his success by commitment, drive, an eye for detail rare in one so skilled at delegation, and perhaps, above all, an instinct for effective and aggressive marketing. In some ways this may seem incompatible with his non-conformist background and lifelong beliefs. It may not be easy to square JJ's pursuit of market share to the point of virtual monopoly, and the wealth that such dominance brought with it, with a nonconformist conscience. But it can be squared; indeed it can be argued that his religious belief was a major motivator in his business career. His success created opportunities for employment; the support he provided for his workers led to a healthier, better educated community; the emphasis on self-help implicit both in the educational system he established and in much else he set up encouraged the acceptance of personal responsibility. This must have seemed to him God's work; indeed in notes he made for a speech in 1872 he wrote: 'it is by taking religion into everyday life and by so acting that the world around us sees that in party strife, or in commercial enterprise we do that, and only that which is consistent with our Christian profession'. And, of course, the acquisition of wealth provided the opportunity to make generous provision for the

115

community as a whole. In 1851 he had started his diary with a rather remarkable set of sentiments for a twenty-one year old:

> 'Another year has opened on my life. I feel how little I have done in the past in what I ought to have done and how much I have left undone. I would mourn it but still look up to my Saviour for his counsel and guidance. May His example be ever before me, teaching and leading me to higher and nobler ends. May I be enabled to do my duty and God's work in all situations in which I am placed'.

He was himself aware of the potential incompatibility between his wealth and his religion. His correspondence with his mother, referred to earlier, demonstrates that he was what has been described as a 'reluctant entrepreneur' and his nephew, yet another Jeremiah, appointed a director at Carrow, recorded his surprise at the 'unbusinesslike demeanour' of JJ, describing him as soft-hearted, deeply religious and as a man 'whose trustfulness, simplicity and kind-heartedness were apparent' and acknowledging that he had done more 'than anyone else to gain for the firm a reputation for generous and considerate treatment of staff'.

The *Descriptive Account of Norwich* quoted at the start of this chapter goes on accurately, if verbosely, to describe JJ as 'a gentleman in whose personality the characteristics of an unfaltering progress and an untiring energy have gone hand in hand to the accomplishment of great deeds in industry and trade, and one who, notwithstanding the close attention demanded by such an undertaking as that now chiefly under his control, has found time to engage in spheres of activity outside the pale of his own immediate business'.

Perhaps the last word should, however, belong to his daughter: 'In business, as in all else, he was scrupulously honest and fair in his dealings. Although he paid great attention to detail he was confident enough of the men he chose as his managers to delegate much operational control. If there was a weakness it arose from his gentle nature.'

Postscript

Colman's continued to be a wholly owned family business until it went public in 1935. In 1938 the firm amalgamated with the firm Reckitt & Sons (originally a Quaker family business) to form Reckitt & Colman. In 1995, Colman's was purchased by Van den Bergh Foods, a part of Unilever. It is pleasing to think that both JJ and William Hesketh Lever would have approved of the link; they were certainly like-minded and truly enlightened nineteenth century entre-preneurs.

[1] When, while undertaking the research for this Chapter, I came across this unusual name it seemed familiar. It transpired that my great grandfather, the High Church Vicar of East Dereham, responsible for the National School there, did not agree with Colman's view of Synge, recording in his diary on August 3rd 1870 'The new (H.M.) School Inspector Rev. Mr. Synge came. Alas! What a difference from his predecessor Mr. Meyrick. This man is one of the most objectionable style of clergy, in comparison with which one could embrace the evangelicals. He was full of self-importance & conceit'. Synge also crossed swords with Caley. Synge was Vicar of St Peter Mancroft at the time of Caley's expansion of the factory. The buildings adjoined Synge's vicarage and he complained about the loss of light and privacy.

[2] This means of communication was tested on the 11th November 1878, in cooperation with the Great Eastern Railway, beside whose line the telegraph wires ran. The equipment was provided by Edison's, an American company, whose representative, Mr Adams, was directing affairs at the Norwich end of the experiment. The first attempt was at 4.00 pm and proved unsatisfactory. Because it was felt that the 'crackling and bubbling sounds' which prevented effective communication were brought about by the heavy use of the wires for traditional telegraphic messages at that busy time of day, it was determined that another attempt would be made at 9.00 pm. This proved slightly more satisfactory in that there was sufficient clarity for Mr Adams's American accent to be distinguishable in London. A few words could be exchanged and, in the

English manner, these focussed on the weather, it being agreed that, at the time of the earlier attempt, there was a sleet storm in progress at either end of the line. This was believed to have been an additional cause of the poor reception. The cornet player, in the Norwich office, then took over. There was an interesting sequel to this experiment. The Bell company, rivals of Edison, claimed that the equipment used in the experiment infringed their patent rights, and Edison had to develop new equipment.

Sources

Carrow Works Magazine, October 1920/1925/1926

The Advertising Art of J & J Colman - Yellow, White and Blue (internally produced c.1977)

The History of J & J Colman, S. H. Edgar, unpublished but held in the Unilever archive

Enlightened Entrepreneurs see bibliography

Jeremiah James Colman, a memoir by his daughter, privately published 1905, The Chiswick Press.

Norwich, a Social Study C. B. Hawkins, see bibliography

'Souvenir of a visit to Carrow Works' printed by Fletcher of Norwich 1901.

Norwich since 1550 see bibliography

The Nineteenth Century Open University East Anglian Studies: see bibliography

Record of a Memorial Service commemorative of the death of Mr J. J. Colman 'for private circulation', held at The Norfolk Record Office, Anon, published September 1898 and held at the Norfolk Record Office

Colmans of Norwich, Information Guide No 3 produced by Unilever Archives and Records Management.

'Cleanliness Next to Godliness: Christians in the Victorian Starch Industry' Roy Church & Christine Clark, published in *Business and Economic History*, Volume 28, No.2 Fall 1999.

A Descriptive Account of Norwich, see bibliography

'Mustard and Starch' from *The Grocer Magazine*, April 1862

Albert Jarman Caley (18291895)
Chemist, Mineral Water Manufacturer, Chocolatier and Philanthropist

'We, the undersigned, who have had the privilege of serving you, desire to express our deep regret at your retirement from business. Some of us have worked for you over a quarter of a century, all of us wish we could serve you longer.'

Illustrated address to A. J. Caley from his staff on the occasion of his retirement.

Albert Jarman Caley was one of twelve children. He was born in Windsor, where his parents owned a store that later became a part of the John Lewis chain – the premises are now occupied by a branch of T. K. Maxx. From 1841 to 1844 he was educated at Eton College, and in 1855 he married Elizabeth Bain, the daughter of a bookseller. The wedding records describe the bridegroom's father as an 'Esq.' which suggests that he may not by then have been actively engaged in the family's retail business. The officiating minister was a Rev G. A. Caley, presumably another family member.

Eton College's records show Albert and Elizabeth later residing at 1 Haymarket in St James's - which was in fact the business address of Elizabeth's father, so presumably they were living 'over the shop'. Bain's in the Haymarket was something of an institution[1]. Despite these London and Home Counties origins Caley had a longstanding connection with West Bradenham in Norfolk (well known as the home of the Rider Haggards) where his family seem to have held land for many centuries. Although he is recorded as being resident in West Bradenham as early as 1852, his eldest child was born in Windsor in 1857. Caley must have moved very soon after the birth to Norwich because, having qualified as a pharmaceutical chemist five years earlier, he opened a chemist's shop in London Street Norwich in the same year.

Some time later he took a partner, the splendidly named Octavius Corder, who was still engaged in the chemists' shop in London Street as late as 1904. While Corder concentrated on the pharmacy, Caley was able to experiment with the manufacture of mineral water, beginning in a very small way, in the cellar of his London Street premises in 1863. In the meantime he and Elizabeth had two further children, Mary and his son Edward, born the previous year, who was to join him in the business. Four more children followed, but three died in infancy.

Mineral waters may seem a strange diversion for a chemist, but in fact the business logic was impeccable. In those days medicines were not in tablet form, and many remedies were dispensed, of necessity, in a potable solution. His waters were an immediate success, and within a year he had to take additional premises in nearby Bedford Street to accommodate the demand from both doctors and other chemists.

The business continued to expand rapidly and in 1879 he took over a former glove factory in Chapel Field, a location at which the company stayed until its final closure in 1996. This was a convenient location for Caley, literally across the road from his home in The Crescent, an area that even today is a haven from the bustle of the city. He lived there quite modestly; the 1871 census shows the family as having just two servants, about the norm for families in such a solid middle class area. At this stage he was still listed as a pharmaceutical chemist.

He was still living in The Crescent ten years later, but now described as a Mineral Water Manufacturer. The progress of the company can be traced by reference to his occupation as shown in succeeding censuses – by 1891 he was listed as a Manufacturer of Mineral Waters, Chocolates and Cocoa. He had moved, but was still close to the factory and his two daughters, still then unmarried in their 30s, lived at home. Edward, however was married and living independently with his wife and two servants. By the time Edward was 19 he was already listed in the census (1881) as a manufacturer of mineral waters, so clearly he was not expected to train for a profession as his father had, although 'in later years' he is said to have 'qualified himself by the study of chemistry'.

From the first it was clear that Caley was imbued with an entrepreneurial spirit. *The Grocer Magazine* in a 1905 retrospective described him as 'a man of enterprising and active character'. He certainly had both courage and vision. His move to Chapel Field could not take place until he was confident of the water supply. For this he had to drill down over 300 feet to locate a suitable supply. Then an entire year was taken up pumping the water to remove any impurities. It wasn't until 1880 that the first bottling could take place and Caley could be confident that he had found the right site. He certainly had. Nearly 50 years later Lincolne Sutton, the Public Analyst for Norwich, described the water as being 'of exceptional and bacteriological purity...a water of the highest quality; one more suitable for drinking would be hard to find'. It is no wonder that Caley's later adopted the word 'ARTESIAN' as their telegraphic address.

Chapel Field was, at the time, a good class residential district with beautiful gardens and established trees. The immediate area however was less attractive; an article in the Caley Magazine of the 1930s, written by a Mr Wheeler, who had joined the company as early as 1881, refers to non-existent flower beds and 'a few enclosed trees, planted by well-known people, which never seemed to flourish'. Wheeler goes on to refer to the use of the gravel paths around Chapel Field as a track for penny-farthing races. As a penny-farthing rider himself he was careful to record that although many riders sustained injuries the public were not at risk. The arrival of Caley's, albeit with a small staff initially, must have changed the character of the district significantly. There were disputes about building, drainage and light but these were generally amicably resolved. One particular issue, relating to drainage was not so easy to resolve. A Mr Hawes, a local contractor, wished to build new houses which needed extensive additional pipes passing through Caley's works. The correspondence is an interesting mixture of the aggressive and the polite. Caley consulted his solicitor, Isaac Bugg Coaks (see Sir Robert Harvey) and strong letters were sent. On the other hand, he once wrote to Hawes saying it would be unfair for Hawes to bear the whole cost of repair to one drain, and enclosing 16s.11d, being half the total bill. Whether this was an instance of Caley's magnanimity or an indication of his irritation with Hawes is a matter of conjecture, but the letter was written in red ink!

The scale of the investment in the new factory is amazing for a man whose first enterprise had been a small retail outlet. The investment turned him into a manufacturer on a grand scale with a wide range of mineral water products that had a reputation for purity that made them the choice of princes and potentates. Indeed so impressed was the future George V that arrangements had later to be made to ship Caley mineral waters to all corners of the earth during his world tour in the SS *Ophir* in 1901. Caley was appointed as supplier of mineral waters to Queen Victoria and Edward VII as well as supplying the House of Commons and many clubs in St James's. Marketing techniques employed included the use of personalised branding. An 1890s stock inventory includes a long list of different labels for various clubs, colleges and companies by whom Caley's products could be sold under their own personal brand.

As well as the medicinal products he developed for local doctors and chemists, he had developed a range of flavoured drinks. Caley's were most renowned for their ginger beer, but they also produced soda water, Seltzer water, lemonade, ginger ale, Potash water and cloudy lemonade. All were of the highest quality thanks both to the purity of the water used and the care taken with the bottles; each had to go through the sterilisation process twice before it could be used. Caley even developed a drink using local hops but, as the *Norfolk News* reported, in 1883, 'needless to say it is non-intoxicant'. This was the age of the Temperance Movement. The brewing of ginger beer required the construction of something very akin to a brewery, and a tower was constructed so that gravity could be used to help in the process of removing any impurities. The move into carbonated drinks proved a sensible diversification because the development of tablet medicines spelt a rapid end to the medical market.

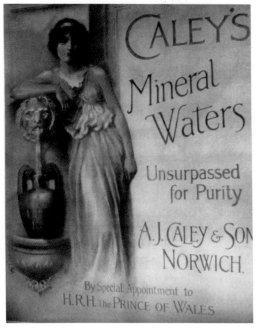

Religion played an important part in Caley's life; he became a member of the Plymouth Brethren, an evangelical sect widely regarded to this day as having an exceptionally strict code, and his Christian beliefs were evident in the way he ran his business.

Working hours in winter were from 0800 to 1900, six days a week. Boys under the age of 18 were, however, given a 'half day' on Saturday – only working from 0800 to 1600. In summer the hours were much longer, from 0400 or 0500 until the work was finished, often not much before midnight. On Saturday nights however, work had to cease by 2355 to avoid working on the Sabbath and it was apparently the practice of Albert Caley personally to 'draw the taps' to ensure that no work was done on the Lord's Day.

Apart from the labourers, Caley initially employed very few staff, handling all correspondence and management processes himself, with the help of his son Edward, and nephew Frederick, who joined the business in 1878. Even though the business was growing rapidly, the office staff in the early days comprised just two clerks, one to keep the day book and the other the ledgers, and another described as a 'manager-representative'.

The manufacture of mineral waters was clearly a complex matter. An annual stocktaking towards the end of the nineteenth century discloses ingredients comprising an eight page list of 'chemicals', three pages more of 'oils', several more of 'syrups' and another four of 'perfumes and tinctures'. No wonder the skills of a chemist were needed to blend them.

The process of manufacture itself was rigidly controlled. By the early 1900s a mechanised system injected the carbon into the water which automatically fed into metal cylinders which were silver-plated to prevent impurities. From these cylinders further machines filled the bottles and siphons, which were first soaked, scrubbed by mechanical brushes and then rinsed with powerful water jets. Despite this high degree of mechanisation for the time, the number of employees grew rapidly, exceeding 700 by the early 20th century.

The differential in working hours between summer and winter serves to emphasise the seasonal nature of the mineral water business. While the manufacture of medical preparations would have remained constant, or more probably increased in the colder seasons, the demand for cold refreshing drinks was clearly greater in summer. This meant that the opportunities for employment were also seasonal and Caley, anxious to provide his employees with regular sustainable employment, found a solution in diversifying production so that the imbalance between summer and winter was ameliorated.

The initial solution was, simply, to manufacture a drink that would be more attractive in the colder parts of the year – cocoa. Cocoa had originally been manufactured by Quaker owned firms, such as Fry's. A remark attributed to Caley was that 'if it could be made by Friends, it could certainly be made by one of the Brethren'.

The initial attempts at manufacturing cocoa and, later, chocolate sound like something dreamt up by Heath Robinson. Mr Wheeler, writing many years later in the Caley Magazine, reported that no-one in the firm knew the first thing about how to manufacture cocoa, a problem only resolved by the agreement of the suppliers of the machinery to provide expert assistance in all stages of the process. To facilitate its manufacture a separate bay had to be built on to the factory. Despite its amateurish initial development the product was launched, successfully, at the Norfolk & Norwich Fat Cattle Show; true to his medical roots Caley produced not just ordinary cocoa, but also a homeopathic version called 'Cocoamel'. More representatives were taken on to sell the enlarged range and they reported a demand for chocolate, which Caley decided to meet. It proved another sound business decision, for chocolate was to become the main product line for the firm. As the *Norfolk News* commented, 'The ingenuity of Mr Caley in endeavouring to cater for the popular taste is remarkable'.

In the initial stages of chocolate manufacture the principles of Heath Robinson were even more evident than with cocoa.

The first experiment in production was described by the same long term employee. The ingredients for the cream were boiled in a saucepan, beaten by hand on a marble slab and poured through the spout of a kettle into moulds. These moulds had been made by the simple expedient of repeatedly pressing a cork into a piece of starch. Once poured into the mould and cooled the mixture was hand-covered in chocolate by an employee who had never seen the process before and who had to learn by trial and error.

Apparently the resultant taste was acceptable because Caley then employed a French chocolatier, M. Olgard, to oversee production. Born in Paris in 1840, Louis Olgard had been chocolatier to the French court. He lived in Heigham with his wife, also born in Paris, and their three sons and four daughters. His eldest son also worked in the factory. They had moved from London where his six younger children had been born. M. Olgard recruited and trained large numbers of female operatives – it was this move into chocolate manufacturing that led to the employment of female staff for the first time in the company's history, although it was still understood that precedence in the appointment of staff should be given to men. The role of the female staff included both the making and the wrapping of chocolates. The manufacturing process quickly became mechanised using steam-driven plant to produce economically, and in bulk, what a contemporary described as 'these admirable commodities'.

There was no refrigeration equipment in the factory so it is probably as well that production in these early stages was only about 50 chocolates a minute, a figure which had increased tenfold by 1996.

The initial experiments may seem amateurish but the results were spectacular. Caley set out to target a market dominated by the Swiss and, as with his mineral waters, the key to his strategy was quality. The milk used was from a local supplier at nearby Whitlingham and was exceptionally pure. Only the very best cocoa beans – from Caracas and brought direct to Norwich by sea – were used and great care was taken in the process of making the chocolate. By the end of the century the manufacture was largely mechanised. Power was provided by a combination of steam for the large machinery and electricity for the small. The cleanliness of the engine room and the burnished appearance of the machinery itself drew from one visitor a rather fanciful comparison with the engine room of a Navy ship. Such was the dependence on mechanisation that between 1887 and 1903 the power used increased from 18 hp to 260 hp.

Presentation was critical too, and great attention was paid to the packaging of chocolates, which was decorative in the extreme. In the 1890s a 15 year old boy turned down the offer of a publishing apprenticeship with Jarrold's, deciding instead to pay a premium of £40 to get one with the lithographers Page Brothers. There he worked an eleven hour day for 2s.6d per week before spending two hours a day extra at the School of Art. His talent was quickly recognised by the Caleys who were customers of Page and he was commissioned to produce posters and designs to go on their chocolate boxes. The apprentice was Alfred Munnings who, in time, became one of the finest painters of horses, enjoying commissions from every monarch from George V to Elizabeth II. He also produced the illustration which was to become the trademark of Bullard's Brewery at the time of Sir Harry Bullard. Not a usual history for a President of the Royal Academy, for such he became.[2]

No wonder Caley's chocolates proved even more popular than their mineral waters, and were exported to Canada, Australia, South Africa and India.

That Caley cared greatly for the welfare of his employees is beyond doubt, despite the hours they worked; they were even expected to work every Bank Holiday except Good Friday and Easter and Christmas Days. He was meticulous about the proper provision of lighting and ventilation in the factory. He encouraged the provision of sport and social opportunities for them – apparently there was a ten minute lunch break in which the boys and men went out for a 'knock' at cricket.

Hand-making chocolates at Caley's

The duration of such games would have made today's 20/20 games look like a timeless Test. While the factory was being developed these games took place in part of the site but when the building work was complete proper facilities were provided, and, where possible, the summer working hours were adjusted to ensure breaks were available in daylight to encourage the cricketers. The employee in charge of these arrangements was a Mr Cowles, himself an all-rounder who played for Norfolk over a period of years with limited success, the high point of his career coming in 1900, when in a county tour of the north east he scored 82 not out against Durham at Darlington, and took 7 for 55 against Northumberland. After Caley's retirement, his son continued to encourage outdoor sport and when Edward too came to retire on the sale of the business he and his cousin left some of the proceeds for the provision of a pavilion for the Athletic Association.

The long working hours in summer were punctuated by occasional slack periods, when employees worked in the gardens; at busy times, when working hours were long, they were allowed to supplement their teas with grapes, fruit and lettuce grown there. During those months, members of Caley's household played tennis in the grounds, but in the winter, if the ground was frozen, employees were given time to skate.

The illuminated address quoted at the beginning of this chapter later referred to the workers' gratitude for 'all you have done for us as our benevolent employer who has ever been mindful of our welfare and happiness'. Even though it went on, with a touch of Victorian overstatement, to refer to Caley having 'made labour sweet by acts of generosity and considerate treatment – a true example of kindness' it was probably a genuine feeling. By the standards of the day, Caley was a model employer.

Caley's benevolence towards employees was, perhaps, at least in part a result of his Christian beliefs. Outside the factory he was a benign influence in the affairs of Norwich. He was involved in the Norwich City Mission, he sat on the Hospital Board of Management and was a supporter of the Bible Society, the Militia Reading Room, the Discharged Soldiers' Society and, perhaps bizarrely for a maker of cocoa, the Soup Society.

His charitable efforts seem to have been targeted at the promotion of the Christian faith and the relief of poverty with an underlying emphasis on 'improvement'. The Norwich City Mission was a non-denominational movement that sought to take the Christian message into the poorer parts of the city, while the aims of the others are, with the possible exception of the Soup Society, self-explanatory. Records of the latter are thin on the ground, the last meeting for which records are available pre-dates Caley's involvement, but the object was to provide warming and nourishing fare for the poor. The need may have been particularly great in Victorian Norwich where poverty was rife as the city began to recover from the loss of its traditional weaving and shawl-making industries. One upside of the poverty, according to a social commentator of the time, was that the level of drunkenness was far lower than in other centres because of the low wages. A less kindly commentator has suggested that it was more a reflection of the weakness of local brews. Soup kitchens were much in evidence throughout the country and extremely popular.[3]

In appearance Caley was described as 'spare-built and benevolent' – indeed an article written after his death said that he would be remembered both for 'his somewhat attenuated form' as well as for his philanthropy. Clearly he didn't over indulge in his own products.

A true family man, Caley remained on good terms with his son, Edward, and, in contrast with the cases of Bignold and Jarrold (qv), there was an orderly and amicable transfer between the generations. Caley retired in 1894 but, sadly, died just a year later. His wife died in 1903.

Caley's obituary described him as 'a good citizen, a philanthropic Christian of broad views and a splendid character as a businessman'. It is only in recent times that obituaries have tended to move from the obsequious to the objective, but even allowing for the Victorian tendency to eulogy, it seems a reasonable assessment. In business he was clearly innovative, forward-looking, willing to take risks and adroit. Some of his business strategies were driven by a wish to provide secure year-round employment for his staff and his charitable activities reinforce the impression of philanthropy. His strong Christian commitment is beyond question, though not all would see the practices of the Plymouth Brethren as indicating a 'broad view'. He would probably have been proud that one of Edward's daughters spent some years as a missionary in Kenya.

His achievement, in the words of *Grocer's Monthly* was to have built a business 'which took its position as one of the great manufacturing industries of the country'. Not bad for a provincial chemist!

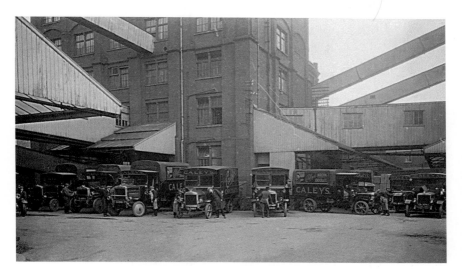

Caley's vans

Postscript

Edward Caley and his two cousins (the second of whom joined the firm after his uncle's death) continued to run the business on similar lines. They invested in mechanisation but sought to reinforce the founder's approach to the mitigation of the seasonality of employment. To do this they introduced, in 1898, a product line that was still an important part of the business as late as 1953 when it was merged with the famous firm Tom Smith, the manufacturer of Christmas Crackers. It seems strange that, by 1918, their letterhead still described the firm as manufacturers of mineral water and brewers of ginger beer – no mention of chocolates or crackers. But they

131

did disclose one new product; they described themselves as cider makers. Edward clearly did not feel the need, as his father had, to live in close proximity to the factory, he is believed to have been living in Cromer at some stage, but had purchased a house, Pine Banks, on the outskirts of Norwich, in Thorpe, by 1911. Coincidentally, in the context of this book, he purchased this property from a member of the Jarrold family, and it subsequently became the Sports & Social Club for Bignold's Norwich Union.

Caley and his son, Edward

In 1918, the Caleys sold the business, by now particularly famous for its Marching Chocolate, a big favourite in the trenches, to The East African and Eastern Trade Association who, in 1932, sold it to John Mackintosh & Sons Ltd of York, perhaps a snip at £138,000. The new owners grew production in Norwich which became the home of such popular lines as Rolo. In 1938 Caley's (the brand was still used for some products) advertised that they had, in the manufacture of chocolate, used enough milk in a year to float a 10,000 ton liner.

Unfortunately during the Baedeker raids of the 1939/45 war Norwich became a prime target and the factory was destroyed by incendiaries in 1942, Caley's own fire brigade having exhausted the supply of water in an attempt to save a neighbouring building. After the war re-building took until 1952 but the factory then re-started the manufacture of chocolate. The mineral water business was disposed of to a local brewer, and the manufacture of crackers was hived off in a merger with Tom Smith.

When Mackintosh's, by then Rowntree Mackintosh, were taken over by Nestlé the new owners decided to manufacture only on one site. The factory at Chapel Field, which was by then producing annually two tons of Rolo and no less than 40,000,000 Easter eggs was closed with the loss of over 1,000 jobs. Later the site became the Chapel Field Shopping Centre. The Caley brand was purchased by a group of former managers in the company whose original intention was to manufacture in Norwich's appropriately named Sweetbriar Industrial Estate, but today Caley's is part of the privately owned Unicheq Group, and its only remaining presence in Norwich is a café situated in the 15th Century Guildhall, which is decorated with reproductions of Caley advertisements from the days of the company's past glory.

[1] In an article in the *Spectator* in 1935 Arthur Waugh (Evelyn's father) wrote 'There was a shop at the foot of the Haymarket where Mr Bain was at home to his friends, and where the purchase of a book had something ceremonial about its dignity'. Amongst the habitués was Lord Rosebery, of whom Bain is said to have declared that 'he knew every luxury of the bibliophile except the thrill of buying what he could not afford'.

[2] There are some interesting dimensions to the Munnings connection. It was a senior Caley's man, John Shaw Tomkins, who was effectively Munnings's first patron, taking the young artist on a number of overseas trips. Munnings painted the scene of the Caley stand at the Leipzig Trade Fair in 1897. His talents were not wasted; Tomkins had Munnings set up an easel in front of the stand, and rattle off Caley posters to attract the attention of passing visitors. The painting of the Caley stand at Leipzig came later into the possession of Lord Mackintosh at auction. Apparently he had sent an agent to bid for the painting who wound up bidding

against another agent, sent by one of the Mackintosh senior management team to purchase the painting for Lord Mackintosh as a gift.

Munnings clearly enjoyed his work for Caley's. In his autobiography he wrote 'I started again on large poster designs for Caley's chocolates. My models were a dark-eyed attractive cousin and a friend. The cousin had beautiful arms and black hair, and was a flirt. Her name was May'.

[3] A Norfolk vicar, gave in his diary a description of a soup kitchen in the 19th century, in London: –
'December 16th. While purchasing some things to take into the country saw a vast crowd of poor persons at a door opposite. It was a public soup kitchen, & the headman very civilly explained everything connected with it. They sell 600 portions per diem, consisting of an excellent pint of pea soup, and a good-sized piece of bread, for which they charge one penny. I'm told they purchase the "waste" from the Clubhouses for this purpose. Nothing could exceed the cleanliness of the place & of the waiters, who, when they handed a ration, & took the penny from the voracious unwashed, passed a wooden ball along a wire, as a tally. The soup coppers were heated by gas. Although many of the applicants were of the poorest class, I could see some citizens there to whom it was no charity, and the thought immediately suggested itself that when soup is sold, even at a nominal price, there is no means of preventing the abuse of a superior class availing themselves of a privilege they do not need, & which was not intended for them. The manager of the kitchen confessed to this'.

Sources:

'A Great Norwich Industry' in *The Norwich Annual* 1939
'A man of enterprising and active character'. *The Grocer Magazine, 1905*
Material held in the Caley archive at the Norfolk Record Office
Material in the Joyce Gurney-Read archive at the Norwich Millennium Library,
Men who have made Norwich, see bibliography
Norwich Adventure privately published by Eric D. Mackintosh
Romance Land by Herbert Leeds published c.1928
The Early Days at Caley's by E. Wheeler, published in *The Caley Magazine* April 1935
The Grocer Magazine
The Norfolk News (24th November 1883),
The Old Etonian Association
The Spectator Archive.
Under the Parson's Nose , see bibliography
'A man of enterprising and active character'. *The Grocer Magazine, 1905*

Sir (Samuel) Morton Peto (1808-1889)
Railway Magnate, Member of Parliament, and Good Employer

We do not hesitate to say that quiet persons all over England are at this moment poorer by millions sterling in consequence of what Sir Morton Peto helped to do...

The Spectator, October 1866

Many in East Anglia will think of Peto, who developed Lowestoft both as a port and as a resort, and who bought and re-built Somerleyton, as a man of Suffolk. Born in Surrey, apprenticed and working initially in London, constructor of Nelson's Column, builder of the Houses of Parliament and railway contractor throughout Britain, and in Australia, Canada, Denmark, Russia, France, Algeria, Portugal and the Argentine, he is not an obvious choice for a collection of essays about significant Norwich figures of the nineteenth century. Yet he lived for some time in Bracondale; he represented Norwich in Parliament for seven years and was responsible for the expansion of the rail network in Norfolk thus changing the county forever. He has earned his place.

The Times, on July 31st 1847 carried a report under the headline ELECTION RIOT. It reported that, on the previous day, polling day, a group of 200 navvies, employees and supporters of Peto, having 'as is their wont, regaled themselves too plentifully with ale' paraded round Norwich waving their hats and giving loud cheers for Peto, until the poll closed with their hero the victor. Their behaviour, reported *The Times*, so incensed the 'Norwich mob' that a riot ensued in which the mob, armed with 'sticks and bludgeons' took on the 'half-inebriated' navvies armed with stones who were driven to take refuge in a nearby Inn, whence they were rescued by the police and taken by omnibus to the station to be put on a train to Ely.

The fact of the riot is not in dispute, but there are at least two versions to just about everything else in the story. Even the date is at issue, some saying that the riot was on the eve of polling day, not on the day itself. Another paper reported that it was not the mob, but supporters of another candidate, Mr Parry, who clashed with the navvies, that the navvies routed them so that it was they who had to take refuge in the inn, not the navvies. Yet a third report claimed that the clash was between the navvies and a group marching for Parry, led by a band, and that it was the band who bore the brunt – one navvy, it was claimed, having jumped through the big drum, destroying it. Both the latter stories say that Peto bore the cost of the damage, some £70. It would appear possible that press reporting may have reflected the political leanings of the proprietor – *plus ça change*.

Whatever the truth about the riot, Peto won the election. Two seats were being contested, with one of the sitting members, the Marquess of Douro, sponsored by Sir Robert Harvey (q.v.), standing in the Conservative interest, Parry, sponsored by J. J. Colman (q.v.) and Peto, sponsored by Birkbeck, a partner in Gurney's Bank, standing as Whigs. *The Times* reported (21st July 1847) that Peto 'as is well known, has achieved a princely fortune by energy and strict integrity, and is in many respects a most eligible candidate for a city which, like Norwich, has fallen from its ancient high estate'. But Peto was not a universally popular candidate. Well known for his espousal of Free Trade and his Baptist faith, his views were lampooned in an election poster in the form of a mock Peto election address. This document included such gems as a feigned regret that the Cathedral and its grounds might have to be destroyed to make room for a terminus for a new railway, and attributed to Peto the following sentiment: 'I am for free trade in everything but particularly in railroad shares and I anticipate the greatest advantages will ultimately accrue to all classes of the community in general, and to the contractors in particular, from the railroad extension measures'. Described as the 'Great Telegraphic Necromancer' who, 'when walking, made a whistling noise resembling that of a railway' he acquired the nickname Mr Nogo – believed to have been derived from a strong local beer called Nog. Satire was alive and well long before the 1960s.

Once elected, Peto did not, as he had said he would, ease up on his commercial activities to devote himself the more to representing the interests of his constituents. He was nonetheless re-elected in 1852, resigning in 1854 when he suggested and undertook the building of a railway in the Crimea[1] to facilitate the movement of troops and supplies to support the siege of Sebastopol, which had got totally bogged down. The railway greatly improved the situation and Sebastapol fell in September 1855. Peto had offered to build the line at cost; it was this gesture that earned him his baronetcy, but he had to stand down from Parliament at that time as it was not permitted to undertake such a Government contract and continue to sit as an MP.

As an MP he is perhaps best remembered for a Bill he introduced in 1861, having by then become member for Finchley, to enable the burial of dissenters in Anglican graveyards – a proposal which met with much resistance, and was rejected. Indeed most of his parliamentary activity would seem to have been in support of interests he held dear such as the advancement of Baptist causes and the improvement of employment conditions for the working man.

Some felt that his motive in standing for Parliament was to provide himself with business contacts and to enable him more effectively to influence legislation relating to railway developments. Although he was not the most regular attender in the Commons, when he finally stood down in 1868 following his bankruptcy, his departure was noted with regret

S.S. Prince of Wales sailing from Blackwall, carrying navvies for the Crimea

Building the railway in the Crimea

by both Disraeli and Gladstone, acknowledging the scale of his contribution to the development of the railway system and the improvement of the lot of the working man. Indeed arguably his most significant parliamentary intervention preceded his election as an MP and related to his evidence to the Select Committee on Railway Labourers in 1846. In this he drew attention to the poor treatment meted out to many and contrasted this to his own practice of ensuring regular wage payment in cash, and taking care of the spiritual needs of his workers. On one contract he employed no less than eleven men to read the scriptures to the working men. He also built accommodation for them, set up sick-pay schemes (intended to be self-funding, but occasionally topped up by Peto) and arranged for the provision of bibles to those capable of reading them.

At Norwich Thorpe station there is a bust of Peto accompanied by a plaque describing him as 'Baptist Contractor Politician and Philanthropist'. The order in which these are placed is interesting, but the whole suggests just one side of the story. He was not another Colman, to whom three of those epithets could also be applied. There are connections: he attended the same chapel as Colman, the Peto 'omnibus' transporting his family and servants to the Sunday service was large enough on occasion also to accommodate the Colman entourage, returning to their neighbouring home at Carrow House, and Peto's work in bringing the railway to Norwich facilitated the development of Colman's as a national and international business.

Like Colman, Peto was a good employer, in his case maintaining excellent relations with a class of employee generally regarded as being ungovernable, the railway navvy. Like Colman he had a genuine concern for the welfare of his staff, like Colman he created a huge amount of much-needed employment, like Colman his reputation and business interests spread far across the globe and like Colman he gave

139

generously in the public interest, especially where it was aligned with his own. But there the similarity ends. No one would describe Peto as they did Colman, as 'a reluctant entrepreneur' or as 'scrupulously honest and fair in his dealings', and unlike Colman he did not die a wealthy man. It was not just Peto's feats of structural engineering that caught the eye; he was as engaged in, if not so adept at, financial engineering as well. And although as quick as Colman to recognise the value of marketing, Peto was more concerned with promoting Peto than anything else – Peto *was* the brand.

Sir Samuel Morton Peto

Peto's ability to identify with his workers and their consequent respect for him, arose from his having personally experienced the tough and demanding physical work that was their lot. The son of a Berkshire farmer, Peto was born in Surrey and was apprenticed at the age of fourteen to his uncle, Henry Peto, a builder and public works contractor. He was expected to learn the hard way, working in the carpenter's shop before moving on to bricklaying. This hard physical labour was overlaid with the more cerebral. In the evenings he attended technical school, acquiring skills in technical drawing and architectural design. Later in life he was proud to boast of his ability to lay eight hundred bricks a day. His stock with the other workmen was enhanced by a cheerful willingness to do his share of the manual work, and by his assistance in writing correspondence for those of his colleagues incapable of doing so. His progress was such that, by the end of his articles, he was entrusted with the role of foreman on some of the contracts.

As his apprenticeship finished, his uncle Henry died, childless, leaving his business jointly to Peto and to his existing partner, Peto's cousin, Thomas Grissell. Henry Peto's death was not expected. On a trip to Great Yarmouth with Morton Peto (as he preferred to be known) to investigate building opportunities for developing the holiday trade, Uncle Henry had sustained an injury that led to his death some weeks later. Eyebrows were raised within the family at the terms of the will; it had been drawn up just a few days before death, with only Morton Peto and Thomas Grissell present except for a witness and the deceased's lawyer. There was a suspicion that the two might have exerted some pressure to further their own ends. The will was unsuccessfully contested. The estate was of sufficient size to produce an income of £12,000 p.a. although the net income was much diminished by mortgage payments of over £7,000 and annuities of a further £3,000 p.a. The business, though large, was therefore quite heavily mortgaged and it had had a rather chequered history. Having won a number of major contracts, to build an extension to the Old Bailey, the Royal

Naval Hospital at Great Yarmouth, the London Custom House and others, it suffered a major loss in reputation when, in 1824, the central part of the Custom House collapsed. The cause of the collapse was shoddy building work, especially the failure to provide adequate piling to support a structure built on poor subsoil. Henry, though not wholly to blame, was found to have acted in a way 'inconsistent with the character of a fair and responsible tradesman'. Claims and counter claims enriched the legal profession for some years before a settlement was finally reached after Henry's death.

Despite this reputational damage the company continued to attract good contracts, and this continued after Henry's death. Morton Peto showed his mettle shortly after he inherited with a spirited and humorous response when challenged by the Earl of Devon that he looked too young to be entrusted with the commission to rebuild Hungerford market, for which he had tendered. He met the challenge by offering to send Thomas Grissell 'who looked old enough for anything' or alternatively to acquire some spectacles so he could appear older. Whether it was the humour, the confidence of his presentation or just the competitive nature of his tender, £42,000, Grissell & Peto were awarded the contract. Further commissions followed, both in London and elsewhere. The pair built the Lyceum theatre, two London churches and rebuilt King Edward VI School in Birmingham. They also built the Reform Club, of which Peto later became a member.

Grissell & Peto were clearly held in high esteem; they won some important commissions, the construction of Nelson's column and the building of the new Houses of Parliament among them, but, by the time they were building the latter it had become clear that the partners, while remaining on the best of terms, saw the future in different ways. Peto identified enormous potential in the development of the railway system, while the more cautious Grissell saw mainly risk. Grissell preferred to continue in the completion of building contracts and, in 1846, the partnership was dissolved, Peto taking on the existing railway contracts and Grissell the rest. Peto then went into partnership with Betts, his brother-in-law.

Grissell's antipathy towards railway work may have increased as a result of the partners' experience on one of their first significant rail contracts, the construction of the 300 yard long Hanwell Viaduct for Brunel's Great Western Railway. This was a prestigious contract but there were plenty of snags. The first of these was the attitude of Brunel's resident engineer, a Mr Hammond. Having made difficulties about the colour of the bricks, he turned his attention to the colour of the mortar, insisting that this should be red, as were the bricks. Peto's response was not untypical: he instructed his foreman to ensure that, on Brunel's next site visit, the great man saw time being wasted mixing cochineal with the mortar to get the required colour, and that he should be told this was the result of Hammond's instruction. Brunel promptly put an end to the practice. But Hammond's foibles were mere irritations compared with what was to follow.

The GWR proved a tardy payer. Peto's relations with Brunel became strained because, although, as chief engineer and arbitrator of disputes relating to the financial aspects of the contract, Brunel finally arranged for Peto to be paid almost the full amount due, he did so in a manner which tested Peto's patience. Every item had to be analysed, usually in the evenings, and at Brunel's convenience. Sometimes Brunel simply kept Peto waiting long after the appointed hour. Peto complained that Brunel treated him in an 'overbearing and inconsiderate' way. Writing to his son, Peto recalled an occasion when, with an appointment for 7.00 p.m., he had still not been seen at midnight.

Peto's involvement with Norwich springs from his building of the railway and his election as MP for the City. His generosity was more directed to Lowestoft, London and national projects.

As far as the railway was concerned Peto had already dipped his toe into Norfolk waters before the split with Grissell. One of their earliest contracts had been for the Great Yarmouth to Norwich line, completed in 1844. Even on this relatively modest contract, 1500 men were employed. And 'employed' is the right word. Traditionally, railway contractors sub-contracted the physical work to others. Peto was different. He deplored the traditional means sub-contractors used for remunerating navvies, by part payment in tokens which could only be exchanged for goods, often shoddy and uncompetitively priced, in shops run by the sub-contractors themselves, who thus developed an additional source of profit. Peto paid in cash. Even when it was necessary for him to use sub-contracted labour (as in this case) he always laid down a condition that the sub-contractor must also pay his men weekly, and in cash. Further he outlawed the common practice of gangers (those in charge of a team of navvies) supplementing their own income by selling beer at a profit to the men. Clearly there was a safety issue in the consumption of alcohol but it was not this that concerned him. It was the gangers' source of profit he outlawed, not the consumption of beer – 'a man has a right to bring a gallon with him if he likes' he is reputed to have said.

Even at this early stage financing railway expansion had become inextricably entangled with the actual building of the line; Grissell & Peto had to agree to take much of their payment for this line in the form of securities issued by the railway company itself instead of cash. The continuation of this practice inevitably created liquidity problems later – perhaps the proximate cause of Peto's failure, and it may well have contributed to Grissell's sense of unease on the concentration on building railways.

To explore, in detail, the labyrinthine passage of Peto's involvement in contracts over the following years is beyond the scope of this chapter. There would not be a ball of string long enough to enable one to retreat and emerge safely from a confrontation with such a financial Minotaur. Suffice to say that, as contract succeeded contract, so crisis followed crisis. Peto had moved irrevocably from the role of pure contractor, adding that of financier and director of the railway company, on several occasions its chairman. Such Board appointments were generally the result of financial difficulty. These were the days of 'Railway Mania' when the whole world and its wife wanted a slice of the action as new railways were planned regardless of their viability. The price of railway shares soared, new shares were issued on a part paid basis encouraging speculation and creating a bubble which, like all bubbles before and since, eventually burst.

Peto himself told his (by then, Bristol) constituents that 'they must be very ill-informed if they fancied railways were to be made with real capital fairly provided in good round sums by genuine subscribers'. This speech was reported in *The Times* (25th April 1868) and the article went on to describe 'Contractor's Lines' which the writer defined as 'lines projected and undertaken not because the district wanted a railway, but because the contractor wanted a job'.

Financing railway development was not a job for the scrupulous. George Hudson, 'The Railway King', who was associated with Peto in a number of enterprises and whose accounting practices were even more suspect, didn't just share the stigma of bankruptcy with Peto, he wound up in a debtor's prison and died in penury.

Peto had contracts all over the world. Perhaps one of his greatest misfortunes was in Canada, where he under-estimated the difficulties caused by the terrain while working on the Great Trunk Railway, tendering at too low a price. His difficulty was compounded by the usual difficulty in raising the finance; the more volatile non-voting 'B' shares did not find a ready market and were effectively dumped on Peto, who had also to agree to take 50 per cent of his contract price in bonds and more 'B' shares. The price of the shares collapsed, costs greatly exceeded estimates, and the company eventually went into liquidation.

Back in Norfolk, Peto extended the Yarmouth/Norwich line to Brandon for the Norfolk Railway, and on from Brandon to provide a link via Ely and Cambridge to London for the Eastern Counties Railway. This latter contract had its own problems with an apparent (and to Peto costly) mis-understanding about whether the line was to be single or double track. Though built in good time – earning Peto a bonus – there were subsequent disputes about the ancillary work he did; his costs for building the station at Cambridge, for example, were a massive five times those anticipated.

The various lines he built in Norfolk had an enormous impact on the county's trade. Within three years of the completion of the Yarmouth line the port was annually sending over 300,000 baskets of fish to London by train and over 40,000 more to other parts of the country. The nature of agriculture changed too – over 30,000 cattle and 80,000 sheep were sent to the London markets in 1847 alone.

Peto also built for the Norfolk Railway a series of branch lines, linking Fakenham, Dereham and Wymondham. He persuaded the company to invest heavily in his projects for the development of Lowestoft, and this leveraged their difficulties when the bubble burst. Owed about £1,000,000 by the company he was appointed to the board, which he subsequently chaired. A parallel appointment as chairman of the Chester & Holyhead Railway followed, again because of the precarious financial position of the company.

He was becoming ever more deeply enmeshed and, in 1857 a pamphlet, entitled 'Petovia', was anonymously published, attacking Peto in the strongest terms. Its frontispiece read:

PETOVIA:

BEING A REVIEW OF THE SCHEME FOR A
RAILWAY FROM PITSEA TO COLCHESTER,
AND AN EXPOSURE OF THE MOTIVES WHICH PROMPTED IT,
THE ABSURDITIES WHICH CHARACTERISE IT,
AND THE INEVITABLE FAILURE WHICH AWAITS IT.
DEDICATED TO ITS PROMOTERS AND THEIR VICTIMS
BY
A TOOTH OF THE DRAGON

It claimed, in 63 biting pages, that 'The prospectus abounds in unfounded statements, fallacious promises and transparent lures; the list of subscribers to the contract is a mass of deception, to gull the unwary capitalist, and evade the spirit whilst complying with the letter of the requirements of the Legislature; and the conviction which forces itself upon my mind is the alternative one, that Sir S. M. Peto, in his concoction of so bald a specimen of railway humbug, must either have been blinded by previous miraculous successes, or rendered desperate by circumstances of a converse character'.

With much detailed financial analysis, 'A Tooth of the Dragon' contends that even if 90 per cent of the conclusions at which he has arrived are mistaken 'there will still remain abundant evidence to convict a man of more mark than Sir Samuel Morton Peto of the commercial vice of affixing a fraudulent brand upon his commodity, and of the moral offence of bad faith towards others, in his sinful lust after the mammon of unrighteousness'.

Speculation about the authorship of the pamphlet has focussed around the directors of the ECR. The new railway would diminish their traffic because it would effectively create an alternative route to London from Lowestoft, cutting out the need to use lines belonging to the ECR, so it may not reflect a widely held view of Peto. If it was written in the interests of the ECR, it worked. The Pitsea project was dropped in consideration of the ECR dropping its opposition to the rest of the planned development. The remaining work was completed in 1859 and Peto was fêted as a hero.

Financial engineering continued and the final nail in Peto's monetary coffin related to the London, Chatham & Dover Railway (LCDR). This company, formerly the East Kent Railway, had ambitious plans to provide an alternative route into London and to provide an extension of this from Victoria to join the Metropolitan Line at Farringdon Street. The total projected cost approached £9,000,000. The company failed to raise the capital required, and asked for Peto's help. As was becoming usual for him he accepted bonds instead of cash for the early works, but, in 1863, he went much further. He agreed to guarantee the interest on stocks issued in respect of the extension. The share issue didn't go well. Peto tried to obtain loans from the banks, and failed. The company then sold him some land which he used as security for loans which were in the form of bills of exchange of doubtful quality. Peto discounted these (i.e. raised cash against them) at Overend Gurney, a discount house whose impeccable reputation was fading as they began, with new management, to take riskier positions. The house of cards collapsed, and in May 1866 Overend Gurney failed; within 48 hours Peto's firm had to suspend payments. Investigations into the failure of Overend Gurney revealed malpractices in the issue of LCDR debentures, for which Peto accepted blame initially, though he subsequently denied that there had been malpractice. Peto sought to calm the storm, and partially succeeded, by presenting a balance sheet purporting to demonstrate assets totalling in excess of £1,500,000 against liabilities of less than £500,000. In reality his liquid assets were probably between £7,000 and £8,000. A committee of investigation was established by the shareholders and its report identified financial irregularities from which

Peto could not absolve himself, though he wriggled quite effectively for a while. Gradually press reaction turned against him, and the resolve of the shareholders to take action hardened. The board who had, until then, stuck with Peto on the 'sink or swim together' principle, cast him adrift and sued him for the £6,000,000 face value of the shares. Peto was adjudged bankrupt on 3rd July 1867.

Peto had lived comfortably enough. In 1844 he bought the Somerleyton estate, rebuilt the Hall and the Church, despite his Baptist faith, and vastly improved the estate village, providing a school. He lived, perhaps, the dream of the *nouveau riche*, as squire and landlord, although the management of the estate was left largely in the hands of his brother James. The property was sold in 1861. Peto's home in London, for most of the time he owned Somerleyton, was in Russell Square, but in 1860 he moved to 12, Kensington Palace Gardens where, the 1861 census shows, he lived with his wife and family and no fewer than 16 resident staff. He moved on to Carlton House Terrace, but commissioned another house in Kensington Palace Gardens (12A) at a cost of £50,000, moving there in 1863. Three years later it was sold.

Following the bankruptcy proceedings he moved first to Budapest, and then to Paris in the hope of finding opportunities there, leaving his family in a house he had rented in Kent. He returned to England, living in a series of rented properties until his death in 1889 at the age of 80. If not in his old style, he lived quite comfortably. His two marriages provided him with a total of sixteen children.

He was certainly a generous man, but his generosity tended to be at its greatest when the gift was aligned with his own interests. When finance for the Great Exhibition of 1851 was in short supply, Peto made an eye-catching offer to guarantee £50,000, thus attracting the attention of Prince Albert who appointed him one of the financial commissioners of the Exhibition. Peto apparently wrote a cheque for that amount on the spot, following a chance meeting with Henry Cole who was effectually the Prince's project manager for the Exhibition. When Cole reported Peto's gesture to the Prince, Albert's response was to whistle in amazement. 'This', he said, 'will stir others'. And it did. It was Peto's gift that really made the fund-raising achievable. Not only did this serve to increase his standing, his involvement also offered the opportunity for profit. The Exhibition provided the first example of the use of public lavatories. During its course more than 800,000 people literally spent a penny. Peto became the sponsor of Jennings, their inventor, and built public lavatories elsewhere as an investment. He was also awarded the contract to build the railway line that gave access to the Crystal Palace when it was removed to Sydenham.

Much of his generosity was directed to the Baptist Church of which he had become a member when marrying his second wife, the daughter of a prominent Lancastrian Baptist businessman. There can be little doubt that his commitment to the Church was sincere, his financial support and particularly the fact that he cooperated fully when the Church, following his downfall, carried out an investigation into his conduct would seem to confirm it.

Spurgeon, perhaps the greatest preacher of his day, who attracted congregations of ten thousand or more, described Peto as 'a man who builds one chapel with the hope that it will be the seedling for another'. Peto built the chapel at Bloomsbury[2], but he also endowed a school for the education of the poor, and set up a mission to work in the neighbouring slums. To be its first minister he prevailed on William Brock, whom he knew from his time in Norwich, where Brock was the minister at St Mary's (which Peto attended when living there) to move to London. In 1852 he purchased the Diorama, a Pugin-built edifice in Regent's Park, originally designed to display the dioramic views of Daguerre, and converted it into a Meeting House. Not content with that, he also funded the minister, at a reported cost of £700 p.a.

An enquiry held by the Church at the time of Peto's insolvency had, as its main focus his moral and religious character. Its report concluded that he had been responsible for some 'legal fictions', but characterised these, in the style of Wodehouse's Ukridge, as 'normal business practice'. The enquiry concluded that Peto had conducted himself with 'perfect candour, openness and integrity'. Perhaps fearing that such a conclusion might be seen as a whitewash of a generous benefactor, they went on to make three critical comments. First, he had taken on too much financial liability – certainly true. Second, he had assumed too much power. They didn't feel he had abused this power, but they felt that, as a Christian, he should not have accumulated it. Finally, although they absolved him of dishonesty, they felt he should have been careful to avoid the impression of it.

Such conclusions may seem generous; those of others were not so kind. *The Spectator*, in October 1866, reviewed the criticisms raised against Peto, and his defence, detailing the confusion in the affairs of the London Chatham & Dover Railway. The review listed the issues as his having assisted in making book entries implying the creation of non-existent shares, having been involved in issuing debentures on those 'shares', that he was involved too in the over-issue of debentures, and that he retained moneys the company provided to repay these to meet his own account. *The Spectator* characterised the first two actions as pawning non-existent shares, and pawning illegal bonds as though they were legal. Their conclusion was less than sympathetic – 'We do not hesitate to say that quiet persons all over England are at this moment poorer by millions sterling in consequence of what Sir Morton Peto helped to do...'

Peto's actions need to be judged by the somewhat elastic standards of the times. *The Spectator* had further commented: 'When a man like him defends the manufacture of shares as a common proceeding, and the over-issue of debentures by saying they were valueless and he therefore raised money on them, and the stoppage of money entrusted for a special purpose in transitu, the country is evidently in need of some moral tonic, to prevent degeneracy becoming active disease.' Peto was not the only contractor to have such difficulties, and to resort to questionable means to resolve them. He was, however a prime user of them and, as a man who adopted publicly such a high moral tone he was an obvious target.

Peto was a man who attracted strong opinions, both favourable and unfavourable. Even looking back today, this is still true. The several biographies of him differ in their assessments. He seems to have been sincere in his faith and in his concern for the welfare of his employees, to whom he offered the security of cash wages, sick clubs and, on occasion, accommodation. The cynic might say that he was buying good labour relations, and there may be an element of truth in this, but it was nonetheless a style of employment not often seen at the time, and there is much to support the belief that his concern was genuine. He inspired a remarkable degree of loyalty among his men, and their behaviour, with the odd exception, was much at odds with the general perception of navvies. Their demeanour was commended by both the Bishop of Norwich and the Dean of Ely.

He was a philanthropist but, as is usually the case with Peto, it may be thought that his generosity was not unconnected with self-interest. He was a highly effective contractor; he got things done. Sometimes he got them done by sailing very close to the wind. On one occasion, when opposed by a turnpike company, he laid rails across the road secretly at a weekend and then negotiated a compromise with the company from a position of strength. On another he marched some 2,000 of his men, on a Sunday, to ensure, by implicit threat of force, the withdrawal of a competing contractor with his men and equipment who had been delaying work on a line because of a dispute with the railway company concerned. His Baptist principles clearly did not extend to the observance of Sundays when his profit was threatened.

Religious, generous, astute, articulate, hard-working, and a conscientious, inspirational employer, Peto was nonetheless a hypocrite and not above financial impropriety. Despite all these failings he achieved much and, even after his disgrace, retained the good opinions of both Gladstone and Disraeli – one of the few things on which those rivals agreed. Disraeli said of him that he admired his 'enterprise and energy' and Gladstone that he had 'attained a high position by the exercise of rare talents', and that he had 'adorned that position by his great virtues'. In Peto's favour it must also be said that he wasn't one to bear a grudge. When he enticed William Brock to move from Norwich to the new Bloomsbury Chapel he did so in spite of the fact that Brock had not always supported him. In the 1847 election Brock had pointedly withdrawn his support from Peto on the grounds that Peto would not undertake to work in Parliament for the disestablishment of the Church of England, a cause that Brock espoused.

One of his biographers, and not the most sympathetic, describes him as 'a paradox'. To amplify this slightly, one might quote W. S. Gilbert's libretto for the *Pirates of Penzance:* 'a paradox, a paradox, a most ingenious paradox' for, paradox or not, this most remarkable of men was certainly ingenious.

¹ The Grand Crimean Central Railway, as it was rather grandiloquently named, was a remarkable achievement. There are several versions of its story extant, not all of which are consistent, especially in regard to the nature of the stock. Some things are clear however. This enterprise required the employment of 250 navvies, another 120 craftsmen (carpenters, blacksmiths etc) and sundry others. A testament to Peto's care of his workers is that these included 5 doctors, 4 nurses and one person to read the scriptures. Almost all the employees had worked for Peto before and he was able to select from a large number of applicants. The pay was good by contemporary standards, and each workman was kitted out with appropriate clothing for the local conditions. More than 20 ships had to be used to ship out not just the men, but the huge amount of material required to build the 29 miles of track. These included a double track from the harbour at Balaclava to the camp, and single lines on to the batteries where supplies were needed.

The job was completed with great speed. Arriving in February 1855 the navvies set to work and, within two months, had not only constructed a camp of huts for their use while they were there, and demolished buildings in Balaclava to facilitate a base for the railway, but also completed the whole railway network. The ability, in all conditions, to transport supplies of food and armaments speedily and reliably was a significant contributor to the final capture of Sebastapol, in September the same year.

² Bloomsbury Chapel was a remarkable project. Very few non-conformist churches were, at that time, built in prominent positions and Peto set out to change this. The story goes that when he approached the Crown Commissioner to lease the land for the building an objection was raised on the grounds that the architecture of such buildings was dull, lacking spires. Peto is reported to have responded that in that case the new church would have not one spire, but two, and that is how it was built. By the early 1950s both spires had become dangerous and had to be demolished but the church remains an impressive and prominent monument to Peto's generosity.

Sources:
The Times digital archive,
P. L. Cottrell in *The Dictionary of Business Biography* ed. D. J. Jeremy, Butterworths (London) 1985,
The Railway Navvies: A history of the men who made the Railways, T.Coleman, see bibliography
Samuel Morton Peto (1809-1889): the achievements and failings of a great railway developer J. G. Cox, see bibliography

Sir Samuel Morton Peto: the man who built the house of Parliament J. L. Chown, see bibliography

The Railway King – a biography of George Hudson, Robert Beaumont, see bibliography

The Spectator archive

Railwaymen Politics and Money Adrian Vaughan, see bibliography

Samuel Morton Peto: A Victorian Entrepreneur Adrian Vaughan, see bibliography

Sir Samuel Morton Peto Bt: eminent Victorian, railway engineer. Country squire. MP, E .C. Brooks, see bibliography

The Life of Sir Samuel Morton Peto (1809-1889). Adrian Vaughan (Ms held at Norwich Millennium Library)

'Bloomsbury Chapel and the Mercantile Morality – the case of Sir Morton Peto' in the *Baptist Quarterly.* January 1984

King Without a Crown Daphne Bennett, see bibliography

John Patteson MP (1755-1833)
Wool Merchant, Brewer, Member of Parliament, Amateur Soldier & Bon Viveur

'On Thursday last Alderman Patteson gave an elegant entertainment at his house in Surrey Street...'

Bury & Norwich Post, January 13th 1802

John Patteson gave many such elegant entertainments, probably too many for the comfort of his son, John Staniforth Patteson, who spent a large part of his relatively short life paying off his father's debts.

Patteson was the great grandson of Henry Spark Patteson, a Birmingham ironmonger and banker. Today this may seem a bizarre combination but, at that time, there were numerous small local banks in a somewhat under-regulated environment. In fact, in Birmingham where there was no public bank until 1765, it was reckoned that nearly 10% of all tradesmen also operated as bankers, at least at the superficial level as 'retailers of cash' as the author of a late eighteenth century history of Birmingham rather politely describes money-lenders. John's grandfather, also Henry Spark Patteson, followed the same occupations but in Norwich, perhaps because his father had married Millicent Coleburne, the daughter of a Norwich ironmonger in a substantial way of business. Her father had been Mayor of Norwich in 1720.

John's father, Henry Sparke Patteson (he added the 'e' himself) died when John was nine, and his mother, Martha, took John and his younger brother to live with his Uncle John, a wealthy Norwich worsted merchant and weaver, who arranged to build a fine town house in Surrey Street Norwich for the family to live in. It was an impressive property; it was said that having employed a London architect, Robert Mylne, to build him the house, Uncle John burned all the bills so no one would discover how much it had cost.

He also assumed responsibility for the boy's education. There is some dispute about where he received this. Some accounts say that he started at Norwich Grammar School, others that he went to the school in Greenwich where his younger brother was to go later prior to moving on to Eton. Most sources seem to assume that the Greenwich school was, at the time, run by the famous – perhaps infamous – Dr Charles Burney, brother of Fanny and son of the organist at St Margaret's King's Lynn. Burney was, like his father, an outstanding scholar, but also a flawed character. He was sent down from Cambridge for stealing books that he then sold in London as his own. However the assumption that Dr Burney was Head at the time must be incorrect since, although he was later both proprietor and Headmaster, he did not purchase the school until 1793 or 1794, by which time John would have been approaching forty.

Whether he was at the school in Greenwich or at Norwich Grammar is perhaps immaterial because, when he was twelve, his uncle sent him to Leipzig, accompanied by a servant, to complete his education. Martha deluged her son with advice and admonition on everything from brushing his teeth to the need for exercise. The intention was that, in order to be a more effective aide to his uncle when he joined the business, he should develop a good knowledge of

157

German. As this was to be under the tutelage of his uncle's business connections he could also learn more about the woollen export trade and, in particular, reinforce his uncle's connections. It was common practice for Norwich manufacturers to send representatives to the continent, and even as far as Moscow. Neither was it unusual to send young members of manufacturing families abroad for their education in this way – it was good long-term planning. The intention was for him to join his uncle in partnership in due course.

The industry was one in which competition was intense, Yorkshire wool and Lancashire manufacture were growing fast and the assertion, many years later by the City Treasurer, that 'such improvements have been introduced that no fear need be entertained of competition with the manufacturers of other places either at home or abroad' would have rung rather hollow even then. Norwich's dominant position as perhaps the most significant manufacturing town outside London was facing challenge and, as the eighteenth century moved towards its close, its importance diminished. The decline in the traditional weaving and worsted industries was marked, despite encouraging signs earlier in the century as the demand for lighter, cotton, garments had grown. In 1752 a statute was enacted which enabled the import and export of such goods through the port of Great Yarmouth, and manufacturers focussed on accessing continental markets. Demand was particularly high at the annual markets of cities such as Leipzig and Frankfurt so it is not surprising that his uncle placed much importance on ensuring that John knew not just the language, but also the local trade connections. The upturn in trade was, however, not sustainable in the longer term, as Norwich was overhauled by competition from the north.

On his return from Leipzig he served his apprenticeship training as a weaver, gaining the approval of his uncle, whose plan to take John into partnership came to naught because he died in 1774, when John was nineteen. John senior had been a widower, and had no children, so John, a particular favourite, was a major heir, under the sharp eye of his mother. The will was unusual in that, in respect of the business, much responsibility was to rest with Martha. As one of the executors she was to run the business with John and a trusted colleague, John Luke Iselin until 1777, presumably because by then John would have attained his majority. At that point the will offered the executors four options. Of these two were only relevant if John and Iselin had proved incompetent, and this was not the case. Each of the remaining alternatives provided for the admission of Iselin to a partnership, on payment of a capital sum, and it was up to Martha to decide if she wished to continue to be involved in the running of the business herself. Iselin's contribution was to be £3,000, but clearly Uncle John set out to ensure that he could afford it because he separately left Iselin the same sum in his will.

In the period between his uncle's death and attaining his own majority John was not only involved in the business but also began to enjoy the lifestyle his inheritance made possible, engaging in the social delights of London and Bath. Independently wealthy, but with business responsibilities, he was able to acquire a degree of both commercial and social maturity under the watchful eye of his extremely formidable but appreciative mother.

Martha apparently opted to continue her involvement after 1777 and in April the following year John left to spend some time on the continent both with a view to completing his education and to strengthening the partnership's business connections. His travels before settling back in Norwich are engagingly described in his correspondence with his concerned mother, who demonstrated none of the *sang froid* expected today of parents whose children are travelling in a gap year. (To be fair, she had no email, Skype or mobile phone as a means of staying in touch. And just as well, or we should not have the benefit of being able to read their exchange of letters.) Quite apart from her concerns for her son's physical well-being, she was keeping an eye on his expenditure.

By the end of the first month she was writing to tell him that, although the business was doing well, he mustn't be encouraged by this news to 'go on spending as you have began' (sic). She added 'Iselin and I are surprised and vexed at your drawing so fast. Sure you must travel in great state, or always with 6 horses, otherwise the money could not run so fast. You see I can't help expostulating with you though you are almost 23'. This was followed by a letter from his brother the following month in which he warns that Martha 'begins to have fear of the expences (sic) of your journey'.

Soon business began to fall away. By June Martha was feeling 'rather low at the slackness of the business', and 'grieved sadly to see the poor people look so disconsolate for want of employment'. John was doing his utmost to drum up more trade, to little avail. From Lübeck he reported that 'gentlemen in the Swedish trade' were loath to order woollen goods because of changing fashions, though expressing an intention to do so when business looked up. He also visited a customer called Otto who had incurred his mother's displeasure by making no orders, probably as a result of a failure to agree a sufficiently low price. In a rare lapse of good taste she attributed his failure to do so to his being a Jew, who had 'sent all our warpers to blow their fingers' (presumably a reference to their under-employment) and saying she would not 'give a f-rt for his friendship'. A few months later she adopted a slightly different tone, instructing John to ensure that future orders from Otto were not lost even if they offered no profit because 'the keeping the poor servants and journeymen at work will be a sufficient reward for such rich folks as we are'. Furthermore she wanted Otto to supply her with sauerkraut.

Martha's letters were peppered also with advice on both behaviour and health, regularly seeking reassurance about the latter. She worried about how he would cope with the heat, with the companionship of some she regarded as not wholly desirable (one of his companions earned the soubriquet Richard the Rake) and whether he would make a suitable match. There was some encouragement for him to set his cap at Bet Ives, daughter of a wealthy merchant and from a family with a tradition of civic service in Norwich. Unsolicited advice accompanied business updates, family and Norwich gossip and political comment. In response John was soothing, sometimes indulging in a bit of gentle leg-pulling but always respectful and anxious to please. His letters describe the country through which he passed in some detail, but not enough to satisfy the family.

Having finished the first part of his tour in Switzerland, where he spent a while with members of Iselin's family, he set off for Italy. There was still some business to attend to, but this part of the trip was primarily to 'finish' his education. Italy did not entirely suit Patteson; the society was not wholly to his taste. He found the Italian aristocracy a pretty poor bunch and inclined to freeze him out as being 'in trade' and the introductions he had to traders were to those he felt not to be of the first rank.

He started in Turin, where he was said to work all morning and attend the opera each evening, before moving on to Naples, where he met the young John Soane, travelling on a three year scholarship of £60 p.a. awarded by the Royal Academy to enable him to study classical architecture. It proved a sound investment on the part of the Academy, for Soane became perhaps the most fashionable of contemporary architects with commissions such as the Bank of England. But fame and fortune were a long way in the future and £60 p.a. didn't go far; John was not finding it easy to restrict his expenses to £500 p.a. It was, therefore fortunate for Soane that he fell in with Patteson and a number of other English merchants and landowners who, between them, employed Soane as their draughtsman to produce illustrations of the sites they visited. Several of them, including Patteson, became clients of Soane back in England. The group travelled, *en garçon*, to Sicily. Patteson had, in the meantime, written of his disappointment at Rome. He was unimpressed too with many fellow tourists who he felt were simply following fashion, or visiting classical sites for fear of being ridiculed as Philistines if they did not. For himself he reported that he could 'scarce steal five minutes for myself'. All day was spent sightseeing, and he was tired out by evening.

The trip to Sicily got off to a bad start. A lack of wind, and an indolent captain made for an extended voyage. On arrival at Palermo the group were delayed for seven hours before they were able to satisfy both the customs and health authorities. He was disappointed to find so much poverty in a land of plenty, but spent two days climbing Etna – 'I don't remember ever being so tired'. Eventually he became home-sick. He wrote, 'Italy is not worth leaving England for, except to an artist or mad enthusiast after antiquities'. Travelling home was a slow process: he took four months, much of it taken up in promoting the family business.

Back in Norwich, and installed in his uncle's mansion, Patteson began a varied life. Prone to extravagance he was nonetheless a formidable figure in Norwich life. He involved himself with the defence of Norfolk during the Napoleonic wars, gained great civic honours, went to Parliament, first for Minehead and later for Norwich, and invested in the brewing business which still bore his name in the 1960s. A Founder director of Norwich Union's Life Office, he also had a significant role in the dismissal of Thomas Bignold (qv).

Patteson came from a background of civic service. He followed the tradition. He was a member of Norwich Corporation for half a century from 1781, the year in which he married Elizabeth Staniforth, daughter of a rich Manchester merchant. Her uncle, John Staniforth, had married a Suffolk heiress, Mary Macro, who owned Little Haugh Hall near Bury St Edmunds. That marriage was childless and Elizabeth was to inherit the estate, thus adding even more to the growing Patteson assets. Martha had inherited a life interest in the Surrey Street property, but it reverted to John on her death in 1799.

His civic record was one of distinction. Sheriff in 1785, he became Mayor in 1788, following in the footsteps of his maternal great grandfather, Daniel Fromanteel in 1725 and his uncle in 1766. His son, John Staniforth Patteson continued the tradition, being Sheriff in 1811 and Mayor in 1823. It was probably Uncle John who had the most eventful period in office. He was called upon to quell a riot brought about by a combination of high prices and an inadequate supply of food. As his wife had died five years earlier, Martha acted as his Mayoress; before leaving to read the Riot Act he reputedly left his chain of office in her safe-keeping, remarking 'God knows if I shall come back alive.' While Sheriff, John himself was knocked down on election day in 1784. Each candidate had his own polling booth with a no-man's land in between. One side's supporters advanced upon the other and a scuffle ensued. The supporter who had up-ended Patteson was arrested, but released on the surprising grounds that he was 'drunk but respectable'.

Given these incidents and Norwich's radical tradition, it is not surprising that in the aftermath of the French Revolution Patteson was an early supporter of the idea of a part time army. He commanded the Norfolk Loyal Military Association with more than 200 members in 1797. There was a limit to the number and ranks of officers permitted in such a corps, but Patteson overcame this by persuading the Lord

Lieutenant, George Townshend, that the Association's existence depended upon the voluntary support of land-owners who, if deprived of the opportunity to take part, might withdraw their support. Their involvement is hardly surprising; one of the key roles of such a force was the maintenance of order in support of the civil power. Their involvement may not have been sparked by patriotism alone.

Norfolk had been the first county to raise a battalion of militia in 1758 comprising, as a contemporary report put it, 'tall well-looking men, old soldiers but still healthy and vigorous'. But such battalions, despite their similarity with the Home Guard of the 2nd World War, were not just Local Defence Volunteers. In fact they were not local at all for long, being stationed in Hampshire almost immediately after their formation.

In 1796 a supplementary militia was formed comprising 1781 infantrymen and 337 cavalrymen. But all was not well and the formalities could not be completed because Townshend was obliged to terminate the meeting to do so because of 'the tumultuous behaviour of the populace'. In February of the following year Patteson's Norfolk Loyal Military Association was formed, supplemented a year later by another corps 'for the purpose of preserving internal tranquillity'.

The Association was cleansed of those deemed potentially disloyal in 1800 and effectually re-formed in 1803 as the Norwich Volunteer Infantry, still under the command of Patteson, who progressed from Captain to Lt. Colonel. The threat of invasion was being taken more seriously and, despite a chronic shortage of arms, the corps was part of the roster of such groups posted to the port of Great Yarmouth. Clearly Patteson was an effective commander. His battalion was one of the very few which, in 1804, was judged to be 'fit to be employed in any situation to which Volunteer Corps can be called'.

Later, enthusiasm for part-time soldiering grew less as the fear of imminent invasion receded and as allowances were withdrawn or reduced. In 1808 volunteers were offered the opportunity to transfer into the Militia, who were paid even while training, but who had geographically wider responsibilities. Most of Patteson's men did transfer, but many others did not and some units were disbanded. The men of Robert Harvey's Norwich Regiment were unenthusiastic and only a few transferred. Despite this, Harvey attempted to assume command of the resulting combined Local Militia Battalion but lost out to Patteson. This was neither the first nor the last time these two leading Tory and Anglican families would fall out.

By this time Patteson was in Parliament, having negotiated a price of 4,000 guineas for the purchase of a seat for Minehead, one of the rotten boroughs subsequently abolished by the Reform Act of 1832. He said that he preferred not to sit for a Norwich constituency. This may have been a rationalisation; he was only offered the opportunity to do so a couple of months after he had paid for Minehead, which he represented from 1802 to 1806. In 1806 he did agree to stand for Norwich, then havered on the grounds of the expense of doing so until a subscription was raised to meet the costs. Drawing attention to his past service to the city, he appeared in his aldermanic gown and topped the poll. His popularity was fairly clear anyway, his return from Minehead having been greeted with a peal of bells.

In Parliament he involved himself in areas that were of particular interest to him. Even while the member for Minehead, he introduced a petition to the House on behalf of the weavers of Norwich, and later that year was involved in an exchange about brewing, which had by then become another string to the Patteson bow. The latter exchange was reported in the *Bury and Norwich Post* in June 1803:

'Mr Vansittart called the attention of the House to the importation of china-ware from the East Indies and Opium from China. It was proposed to impose a duty on Porcelain imported of 80 per cent. With respect to opium it was also intended to increase the duty, as great quantities, he understood, were used in the adulteration of beer. Mr Patteson (of Norwich) wished to know to whom the Hon. Gentleman alluded. He was concerned in the trade, and he conceived any person highly culpable who used a deleterious mixture, when the ingredients for brewing were at so reasonable a price.'

Other matters on which he spoke included the recruitment of volunteers, and he opposed, in committee, the establishment of fixed prices for corn, favouring a free market approach allowing prices to find their own level. He appears, even then, to have taken a special interest in Norwich affairs, presenting a local petition against the Corn Bill and opposing a Bill relating to the paving of Norwich that he felt the city could not afford.

Not surprisingly as a brewer he opposed, in 1806, a bill to increase the tax on malt, but it is surprising to find him opposed to the abolition of slavery, which seems at odds with the concerns he expressed, during his tour of Sicily, for the lot of those trapped in poverty in a land of plenty.

Elected for Norwich in 1806 he continued to be an active parliamentarian, involving himself mainly in financial matters but voting against parliamentary reform. In 1812 he was defeated by Charles Harvey, and didn't stand again. Overall he seems, given his other interests, to have made efforts to find enough time for his parliamentary duties and to have been a good deal more active than some contemporary members. He did not get preferment, although Spencer Perceval unsuccessfully proposed him for the finance committee.

He appears to have accepted his defeat with equanimity because, two years later, in a letter to Lord Hardwicke he wrote:

'I am now retired from the scene of great action, not into inactivity as my commercial concerns are considerable and my sons come to a period of life as to require that initiation and leading on which cannot be done by any other as well as myself.'

His commercial concerns certainly were, as he had put it in that letter, considerable. As well as the partnership with Iselin, in 1793 he had begun to diversify his interests, first entering into partnership with a brewer called Charles Greeves and then, when Greeves retired, taking over the whole business. It wasn't a large brewery; in 1793 it produced just over 1,500 barrels, a little over 50,000 gallons or about 3 per cent of the total amount of beer brewed in Norwich, and was the smallest of the city's eight breweries. Patteson claimed that his purpose in making this investment was to provide employment for his eldest son, John Staniforth Patteson. As his son was only ten at the time it seems probable that his motivation was more to reduce risk by spreading his investments over a wider range of industries. This would have been a prudent policy; the woollen industry was notoriously uncertain but beer was always in demand. He had at least a headstart in the business; among the assets his father had left him was an inn that he had bought as an investment in 1760, The Black Horse in St Gregory's. John had supplemented this in 1792 with the purchase of another inn in St Stephen's.

Certainly a diversification motive is consistent with the policy he then followed of growing his brewing interests both organically and by acquisition. In 1794 he bought the brewery of James Beevor, a particularly shrewd purchase as the deal wasn't just for the brewery but also for a number of inns in which the beer was sold, as well as malthouses. The following year he bought another brewery, that of the splendidly named Jehosophat Postle, by which time he had grown total production to more than 9,000 barrels, supplying ninety inns. The next year he extended still further, buying Fisher's brewery in Great Yarmouth. This was a significant buy, the premises comprising warehouses, malthouses and storage cellars and an estimated £5,000 worth of stock. His main brewery though was at Pockthorpe, a rather seedy part of the city and the original site of Greeves' business, but he was clearly inordinately proud of it. So proud that, in 1797 he entertained Prince William Frederick, the 21 year old nephew of George III, and later Duke of Gloucester, to dinner there in a large vat that was named in the Prince's honour. The Prince was visiting the city as a Major General with responsibility for its defence, but he set out to enjoy his stay. Quite apart from his dinner at the brewery, he went to the theatre, attended the Assembly, and was given the freedom of the city.

**Steward and Patteson's Pockthorpe Brewery,
Barrack Street, Norwich**

The brewing business continued to flourish, probably dwarfing his other diversification into banking and insurance.

In the five years to 1800, production almost trebled and by then about 150 inns, some several miles out of the city, were being supplied by him. This was a remarkable achievement. The local market itself didn't grow much but his share of it more than doubled in these years to something approaching 40 per cent. As the brewery prospered, so the traditional family business began to contract. Patteson had got his timing right. He was not alone. Others in the worsted industry were channelling their capital into alternative industries such as banking. Brewing was a good choice; his brewery had, by 1800, become the largest in Norwich and had, according to one estimate, a capital value of £140,000, perhaps £10,000,000 in today's value. Two years later the declaration of peace between England and France, temporary though it proved, was celebrated in the market place with six barrels of porter donated by Patteson being used to drink the health of the King.

By the time he started investing in brewing he had already purchased estates at Bawburgh and Colney, and was living well. All seemed set fair, apart from the ups and downs of the worsted business. It is pleasing to think that Martha, before she died, saw him at the height of his success, a leader of the commercial set in the city and accepted amongst the gentry. It was the achievement of all her ambitions for him: success, civic honour and social acceptability.

Sharing his success was Elizabeth, his wife. The estate at Little Haugh was a major addition to the £2,000 she had brought as her original marriage portion – a pale shadow of the £100,000 that would have come as the portion of Bet Ives had he married her, as Martha had hoped at the time of John's travels. The marriage produced seven children, but there was great sadness. Three of the sons died of fever within a few days of each other. All three were buried on the same day; all seven children predeceased both their parents.

Prince William Frederick repaid his entertainment in the vat by standing godfather to one of the children in November

169

1801. The child was named William Frederick, presumably in honour of the Prince, at an afternoon christening at St Stephen's Church. After the ceremony the Prince hurried away to a fête at Houghton.

On the face of it, all was well. The mansion in Surrey Street had been extended to plans drawn up by Patteson's old friend Soane,[1] and was the site of much entertainment. Patteson's acquaintance with Prince William Frederick must have placed him in good stead with Norfolk's best families.

The house in Surrey Street, occupied by Patteson, then by Samuel Bignold and after that by the Norwich Union

Members of these families, travelling into Norwich from their country houses for the social ballyhoo that always accompanied the Assizes, found a welcome in Surrey Street. The house was comfortable enough: 'elegant lodging rooms' and library, drawing room and dining room all 'fitted up in a style which is seldom seen but in the houses of our first nobility'

170

reported a visiting relation. With a domestic staff of nine, the Pattesons entertained in style. Social status was a function not just of gentle birth, but also of substantial wealth and the latter was best demonstrated by exceptional expenditure. Such status mattered to the Pattesons, not least to Martha. This status was enhanced in Assize week 1797 when Prince William Frederick accepted an invitation to stay with Patteson at Surrey Street. When the Prince left Norwich a few months later to take up a command in Kent, Patteson hosted his farewell dinner.

Martha's ambitions for her elder son were substantial, and she did all she could to help him achieve them. There can be little doubt that she was a remarkably strong lady, clearly adept in business at a time when very few women were engaged in it. She seems to have been cautious and thoughtful, and yet she must have been aware that the financial condition of the family was at risk. She would have approved the move into brewing for it is clear from her correspondence that she fully understood both the fragility of dependence upon the worsted industry, and perhaps its future decline locally. At the time she died, in 1799, her son still seemed set fair; she was spared witnessing his later financial difficulties.

By 1816, these were becoming clearer. The economy by then was in disarray following the end of the Napoleonic wars, and Patteson was clearly in trouble. In May that year Elizabeth agreed to the surrender of the financial arrangements made for her comfort in the event of Patteson's death. It transpired that he had anyway been raising funds to meet his outgoings on the security of property that had been placed in trust for her, and had been doing so without the knowledge or consent of the trustees. The exact nature of his difficulties is not clear, though a descendant later made reference to both unsuccessful and capital intensive overseas contracts, probably by the original Patteson & Iselin partnership, and to the failure of a London bank. In addition he had continued to entertain lavishly.

It wasn't just Elizabeth who made sacrifices. His son, John Staniforth, by now in his late thirties, agreed to the breaking of the entail on certain properties so that capital could be raised. In his pomp his father had been proud of the collection of paintings which adorned the wall of the various properties. Some of these he had acquired himself, others had come from the collection of Elizabeth's uncle at Little Haugh, but they had to go to raise funds.

Perhaps more importantly, the holdings in the brewery became diluted. Although brewing had proved relatively resilient in the post-Napoleonic war slump, the costs of that war meant higher taxes. The duty on hops increased 50 per cent in 1801, that on strong beer by 20 per cent the following year, and that on malt more than quadrupled in the early 1800s. Raw materials were costing more, too. The price of malt doubled between 1790 and 1804. Patteson's weathered these challenges well; large increases in the population of both city and county compensated to some extent for any downturn in individual consumption. But the brewery was the major asset. John retired from active involvement in the business in about 1820, but his son, seeking to pay off his father's liabilities sold partnerships in the business, mainly to the Steward family, until he held only a minority of the shares. Even these gave him a very comfortable lifestyle and he followed his father both as Mayor and as Lt. Colonel of the Militia.

At this stage John Patteson's financial embarrassment was clearly either not generally known, or not regarded as a bar to other activities. When Norwich Union's Life Office was set up in 1808 both John Patteson and his son were founder Directors. In 1818, Samuel Bignold (Thomas's son) at the height of the furore relating to his father's behaviour, prevailed upon John Patteson to become President of both Fire and Life Societies. The fact that he was selected by Samuel, and was acceptable to the members, suggests that his own difficulties may not have been widely recognised at that stage. Patteson was chosen for both his ability and for his credibility. He proved a staunch ally to Samuel Bignold during the crisis that engulfed Norwich Union, chairing critical meetings during the extended dismissal process of Thomas and fending off the ambitions of a group of London policyholders to take control. His rewards for this support seem to have been substantial, but insufficient to place him entirely clear of difficulty.

He had sold the 200 paintings from his collection of art at Christie's for the relatively paltry sum of £2,349. The estates at Colney and Bawburgh were sold, and, to cap it all he had to sell the Surrey Street mansion on which his late uncle had spent so much, and an extension to which, designed by Soane, he had funded himself.

The Garden at 'Bignold House'

The purchaser was none other than Samuel Bignold; the house became known as Bignold House and later was used as the head office of the Norwich Union Fire Society for many years.[2] It wasn't just the head office. The company occupied the ground floor, while Samuel Bignold and his family occupied the first and second, and his domestic staff the third. This was not the only benefit he gained from his efforts for Norwich Union. They made him a substantial loan to help tide him over. How substantial is impossible to calculate. Suffice to say that, despite his son's efforts to clear his father's debts, there was still, at John Patteson's death, an amount outstanding equivalent today to around £2,000,000.

His eldest son, as all his other children, predeceased John whose later years paint a rather sad picture of the man who had entertained royalty, had been a highly respected civic dignitary, and a Member of Parliament. He had also been a highly visible individual, cutting a dash both in his military uniform and while out driving in his chariot – the first in Norwich. In addition he had prospered both in his original career and, particularly, as a brewer. Eventually he withdrew totally from both commercial and public life, and received a pension of £50 p.a. from Norwich Corporation as 'a decayed alderman'. Although he lived initially in Mangreen Hall, an imposing house a few miles out of Norwich, he moved eventually to a house in Norwich where he died in 1833.

John Patteson was a man who experienced the highs and lows of life. If not born with a silver spoon in his mouth, he certainly had one thrust there when he was young. At some stages in his career it must have seemed that he was destined to increase that fortune markedly, yet in the end he was reduced to accepting a pension of £50 p.a. He seems to have been fortunate in his eldest son, without whose intervention his financial position could have been a great deal worse, and it is to his credit that his success as brewer enabled that son to enjoy a comfortable life despite his father's difficulties.

He knew personal tragedy. Three of his children died, almost simultaneously in the same outbreak of fever at the ages of six, nine and twelve respectively. One died in infancy, another, Robert, a serving officer in the Army, died on service in Canada. Both John Staniforth and his sister Katherine died the year before their father.

While he had a weakness for high living, he was, clearly, also a more than competent businessman and a powerful manager of issues. The expansion of the brewery represents a considerable feat. The decision to diversify into this field, the speed and manner of his acquisitions, buying simultaneously production capacity and retail outlets, and the astonishing growth of market share, all suggest a sound grasp both of strategic issues and of implementation methods. His strength of character and forcefulness are clear both from his military exploits and his firm grasp of the initiative in the Norwich Union's crisis. His correspondence with his mother displays both a sense of humour and of duty. It would have been very hard to dislike John Patteson, an entertaining companion and a generous host.

Postscript

The Patteson brewery continued to prosper by the combined efforts of John's son and the four members of the Steward family who became involved from 1820. The company became Steward Patteson and Stewards. It continued to expand by acquisition, taking over the breweries of George Morse in 1831, and Peter Finch in 1837 bringing between them more than 130 additional pubs into the fold. Confusingly the name of the company was then changed to Steward Patteson & Co. By the turn of the century they owned more than 500 inns. The partnership was, in 1895, replaced by a limited liability company.

The 1904 Licensing Act, something of a sop to the temperance movement, encouraged magistrates to refuse a renewal of a licence if they believed that the number of inns in the area was more than adequate. This led to a decline in the number of inns nationwide. Steward & Patteson saw over 100 of theirs close, although the compensation was quite generous. These closures proved only a temporary blip and

Steward and Patteson continued to expand by acquisition until, in the early 1960s, they controlled over 1,200 pubs.

But the industry was changing and God seemed on the side of the big battalions. Steward and Patteson agreed to join with rivals Bullards to acquire the tied houses of another competitor, Morgans. This still wasn't enough and, having become a public company in the inter-war years, Steward and Patteson were taken over by Watney's in 1967. Brewing continued at Pockthorpe for a further three years, but the brewery closed in 1970.

[1] These plans were for an additional wing to provide a new kitchen on the ground floor and a bedroom, dressing room and nursery above. Soane also designed two marble chimneypieces for the first floor drawing room of the main house.

[2] This sale was for a price of £6,500. There are one or two curious aspects to this arrangement according to documents in the Aviva archive. These suggest that a contract was made, in 1819, to convey the property to John Cocksedge Bignold, rather than to the Society. Further documents confirm that the Directors took possession two years later, the £6,500 having been paid. Yet the same document (1883) sets out that although the Society had enjoyed uninterrupted possession ever since, no conveyance to them had been ever executed.

Sources:
An History of Birmingham, William Hutton 1783
The English Town : A History of Urban Life. Mark Girouard
The Defence of Norfolk 1793-1815: Norfolk in the Napoleonic Wars, J. Barney
A General History of the County of Norfolk, Intended to convey all the Information of a Norfolk Tour, printed for and by John Stacy, London, 1829
www.historyofparliamentonline.org
Patteson papers held at the Norfolk Record Office
Aviva archive material
Mackie's Annals
Norfolk Beers from English Barley, T. Gourvish
Jacobin City, C. B. Jewson

PICTURE CREDITS

BIBLIOGRAPHY

Books

Armstrong, C . *Under the Parson's Nose* (2012)
Arnott, C. *Britain's Lost Breweries and Beers* (2012)
Barney, J. *The Defence of East Anglia 1793-1815* (2000)
Barringer, C. ed. *Norwich in the Nineteenth Century* (1984)
Beaumont, R. *The Railway King – a biography of George Hudson* (2002)
Bennett, Daphne *King without a Crown – Albert, Prince Consort of England 1819-1861* (1977)
Best, G. *Mid Victorian Britain* (1971)
Bidwell, W. H. *Annals of an East Anglian Bank* (1900)
Bignold, Sir Robert *Five Generations of the Bignold Family 1761-1947 and their connection with the Norwich Union* (1948)
Bradley, I. C. *Enlightened Entrepreneurs* (1987)
Brooks, E. C. *Sir Samuel Morton Peto Bt; eminent Victorian, Railway Engineer, Country Squire, MP* (1996)
Burgess, W. & L. *Men Who Have Made Norwich* (1904)
Chown, J. L. *Sir Samuel Morton Peto; the man who built the Houses of Parliament* (1943)
Clayton, E. G. *The First 100 years of Telephones viewed from Norwich* (1980)
Colman, T. *The Railway Navvies: a history of the men who made the Railways* (1981)
Colman, Helen C. *Jeremiah James Colman – a Memoir* (1905)
Cox, J.G. *Samuel Morton Peto (1809-1889): the achievements and failings of a great railway developer* (2008)
Cozens Hardy, B. & Kent, G. A. *The Mayors of Norwich 1403-1835* (1938)
Gooding, J. *The Life of Alfred Munnings* (2000)
Gourvish, T. *Norfolk Beers from English Barley* (1987)
Harley, Gillian *John Soane – An Accidental Romantic* (1999)
Hawkins, C. B. *Norwich – A Social Study* (1910)
Hawkins & Powell (eds) *The Journal of John Wodehouse, First Earl of Kimberley for 1862-1902* (1977)
Holmes, F. & M. *The Story of the Norwich Boot and Shoe Trade* (2013)
Hudson, W. *An History of Birmingham* (1783)
Jewson, C. B. *Jacobin City* (1975)
Jewson, C. B. *The Baptists in Norfolk* (1957)
Mackie, C. *Norfolk Annals* (1901)
Mantle, J. *Norwich Union – the first 200 years* (1997)
Mathias, P. *The Brewing Industry in England 1700-1830* (1959)
Meeres, F. *The Story of Norwich* (2011)